MW00953241

"This book is a must-read if you're yearning to cultivate a workplace that crackles with purpose and empowers your people to shine. It dives deep into the power of a diversity, equity, and inclusion strategy that flips the script on traditional blame games and fosters trust, accountability, and psychological safety. Jess Pettitt doesn't just preach it; she provides practical tools and strategies to dismantle a fear-based culture and build one where vulnerability is a strength, not a weakness. This book is brimming with actionable steps to transform your leadership style and create an environment where everyone thrives. It's a wake-up call for leaders who want to move beyond fear and ignite a culture unafraid to deal with today's challenges. You should read and implement it — your people and bottom line will thank you."
— **Anton J. Gunn**, MSW, CDM, CSP, keynote speaker and two-time best-selling author

"From addressing cultural clashes to navigating conflicting perspectives, *Almost Doing Good* offers practical tools and frameworks to help organizations thrive amid diversity."
— **Bernadette Smith**, keynote speaker and author, Inclusive 360

"Jessica Pettitt's new book, *Almost Doing Good*, serves as a transformative guide for organizations navigating diversity, equity, and inclusion initiatives. Through a blend of humor, tough love, and practical advice, Pettitt offers a roadmap for cultural transformation, urging leaders to embrace failures as meaningful steps forward and leverage disruption for positive change in the workplace."
— **Amy C. Waninger,** author of *Network Beyond Bias*

"In *What If It Happens?* Jess Pettitt masterfully navigates the intricate landscape of DEI, urging us to confront our biases and embrace curiosity. Her powerful analogies and personal insights not only illuminate the challenges but also chart a path forward for meaningful change. This book is a beacon for anyone committed to fostering inclusivity and understanding in our communities and workplaces. It's a must-read for those ready to transform good intentions into impactful actions."
— **Devin Thorpe,** CEO and Champion of Social Good, The Super Crowd, Inc.

"Jess Pettit not only challenges us to recognize the potential within but also to act upon it with courage and purpose."

"Jess Pettitt is a well-established, seasoned leader in the field of diversity, equity, and inclusion whose mastery of the subject is evidenced in her latest book, *Almost Doing Good*. The book is beautifully written, providing clear, thought-provoking examples of myriad DEI issues commonly (and not so commonly) faced by DEI practitioners across industries. Pettitt constantly reminds us to look deeper (both within ourselves and our organizations) and ask the hard questions that allow us to reach the hidden layers that keep us from holding space and relationships with others. She challenges us to always include our stakeholders, ask more thoughtful and intentional questions, and carve out time and space to be fully engaged with those who reply. *Almost Doing Good* is an absolutely essential read for both DEI professionals and companies that want to transform their cultures to be more diverse, equitable, and inclusive to all."
— **Donna Mack**, MEd, The Disability Diplomat,™ disability access and inclusion specialist, professional speaker, trainer, consultant

"In a world that often encourages a 'head in the sand' approach to challenges, Jess Pettit's visionary perspective shines as a beacon of actionable wisdom. Pettit's invitation to confront the unknown with intentionality, collaboration, and a deep understanding of our shared potential resonates with my own journey of inspiring and educating leaders. Through this book, Jess Pettit not only challenges us to recognize the potential within but also to act upon it with courage and purpose. It's a clarion call to lead with empathy, embrace change, and forge a path toward a more inclusive and sustainable future."
— **Glen Guyton,** trainer, speaker, cultural competency navigator

Jess Pettitt, Author of *Good Enough Now: Doing the Best You Can with What You Have Some of the Time*

ALMOST
DOING GOOD

JESSICA PETTITT

Author of *Good Enough Now*

ALMOST
DOING GOOD

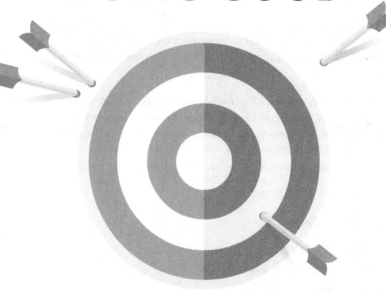

**DOING THE BEST YOU CAN
WITH WHAT YOU HAVE SOME OF THE TIME**

Copyright ©2025 Jessica Pettitt

All rights reserved. The copyright laws of the United States of America protect this book. This book may not be copied or reprinted for commercial gain or profit. The use of short quotations or occasional page copying for personal or group study is permitted and encouraged. Permission will be granted upon request.

For permission requests, write to the author, addressed "Attention: Permissions Coordinator" at 1632 Broadway #420, Eureka, CA 95501.

For information on publishing and distribution rights, call 917-543-0966 or email info@jesspettitt.com

While efforts have been made to verify the information contained in this publication, the author assumes no responsibility for errors, inaccuracies or omissions.

Unless otherwise indicated, all the names, characters, businesses, places, events, and incidents in this book are either the product of the author's imagination or used in a fictitious manner. Any resemblance to actual persons, living or dead, or events is coincidental.

While this publication is chock-full of useful practical information, it is not intended to be legal advice. All readers are advised to seek competent lawyers to follow laws and regulations that may apply to spcific situations. The reader of this publication assumes responsibility for the use of the information. There author assumes no responsibility or liability whatsoever on the reader's behalf of this publication.

ISBN paperback: 979-8-3397618-6-0

Library of Congress Control: 2024917842

Edited by Nancy Graham-Tillman
Graphic design by Nadene Rehnby
Cover design by Summer Stark
Illustrations by Summer Stark, Lush Newton, Devita ayu Silvianingtyas, and Jess Pettitt
Publication coach by Mary Helen Conroy
Photography Sandy Savage
Audio recording assistance by Mike Dronkers

Printed in the United States of America

"Intercultural sensitivity is not natural. It is not part of our primate past, nor has it characterized most of human history. Cross-cultural contact usually has been accompanied by bloodshed, oppression, or genocide. The continuation of this pattern in today's world of unimagined interdependence is not just immoral or unprofitable — it is self-destructive. Yet seeking a different way, we inherit no model from history to guide us."

— **Milton J. Bennett,** *Toward Ethnorelativism: A Developmental Model of Intercultural Sensitivity*

Dedication

Like all of my work, I encourage others to reflect back and see who and how you want to be in this world. This book serves as both the prequel to *Good Enough Now* and a piece of personal therapy needed after working with several clients that were almost-ing so hard that I was getting frustrated.

I raise a tater tot to those that are full of answers and challenge all of us to ask more questions.

* clinks tater tots*

Contents

foreword

by David Rowell, President of Parity Consulting

As a well-experienced DEI consultant, I would not hazard a guess at the number of books I have read on this subject over the years, but *Almost Doing Good* is something special.

When it comes to essential DEI work, this book dares to lead organizations to places they would rather not go — places requiring organizational bravery such as self-reflection and ownership. Using a clear, concise, and wholly actionable model of prepare, recognize, and respond, and coupling that with years of experienced and invaluable expertise, author Jess Pettitt has peppered this book with both the right questions to be asked and the right actions to take in response. And this is not done as a one-size-fits-all compendium.

Too often organizations want answers when they need to ask more questions. And too often organizations want to be handed simple best practices instead of doing the hard work of organizational introspection that would lead to ownership of necessary action. *Almost Doing Good* brings to the forefront critical questions that are far too often left unconsidered in the offices, meeting rooms, and hallways of today's organizations. To fill the void of unasked questions, Pettitt offers sage advice such as "Allow answers to ask questions" and "Be an answer collector looking for the right questions." And she summons her readers to ask questions that (among other things) allow them to:

- Stop and consider with seldom-entertained, action-provoking questions;

- Make no apology for getting straight to the responsibility-centered point with no BS;
- Ask the right questions for necessary organizational self-analysis;
- Let go of assumptions and see through a lens of self-reflection; and
- Acknowledge the obvious (which seldom happens in organizations).

Once they respond to the challenge of rightful questioning, organizations can then embark upon the correct course of action to make the forward-propelling promises of DEI a reality. In teaching them how to do so, Pettitt compels organizations to set aside pretenses around hoped-for simple solutions, such as cheerfully voiced endorsements of best practices. As she states in the book, "There aren't best practices ... but we can learn from what's already been done, and each failure can be a step in the right direction."

Among other things, *Almost Doing Good*

- Normalizes complexity;
- Instills preparatory habits instead of reactionary to-do lists;
- Leads organizations to develop responses, not just reactions; and
- Gives the "why" in addition to the "how."

Filled with case studies and stories, this book makes clear in a no-pulled-punches fashion that "The second-best time to plant a tree is now."

This is a DEI book, and it is not as it is more than that. It is a guide whose lessons transcend DEI practices. For the reader don't read, rather engage with the content, the truths, and own it. Pause and grasp. Stop and reflect often and intently. Carefully consider the facts, stories and questions put forth. And if you do that the book becomes not only a catalyst of improvement for DEI application, not only means to greatly broaden DEI acumen, but also nutrient for professional and personal insightfulness.

— **David Rowell**, The Parity Consultant,
facilitator, trainer, coach and author
parityconsultant.com

Welcome

check-in

On this journey there are going to be unexpected turns, dead-ends, cul de sacs, potholes, and joyous country roads that ramble alongside the efficient path you might be expecting. Along the way, I will check in, offer you a snack, review where we have been, and give you a chance to catch your breath. Then we will begin again. I will use these check in moments to provide a roadmap of where we have been and where we are going. You made it this far and that is great.

Answers That Seek More Questions

"Stop spit-polishing a landmine!" I said louder than I'd expected to as I threw my pen down on the table and pushed my chair back in the CEO's office. Exasperated yet succinct, I'd finally gotten his full attention.

I'm still a little embarrassed by my loss of calmness, but I'd had it. CEO Chuck, not his real name, had the motivation, information, and resources to do something with his organization, but he just couldn't seem to act. It had been over a year since George Floyd's murder captivated the attention of most business leaders, and Chuck wanted to do something but just didn't know what. I'm not certain he could articulate the difference between diversity (D), equity (E), and inclusion (I), though it was emblazoned on the conference room wall as the top value of his organization. Some organizations even add belonging (B), justice (J), and other values to their DEI strategic plans or annual reports, yet most suffer from the same problem. We'd gone round and round in circles about not wanting to take a risk and fail, not wanting to be first at something new, and not wanting to be left behind or caught with his pants down, so to speak.

There isn't an example out there of a business completing a DEI initiative wholly and successfully. It doesn't exist. There aren't best practices, either, but we can learn from what's already been done, and each failure can be a step in the right direction.

I didn't know it at the time, but when I blurted out, "Stop spit-polishing a landmine," it really and succinctly articulated the struggle that connects organizational leadership to countless stalled DEI initiatives. Landmines create a volatile and dangerous situation for everyone in the surrounding area.

In the late 1980s, Princess Diana campaigned against the war practice of leaving explosives hidden across fields where innocent bystanders, animals, and vehicles could accidentally trip an explosion. The solution was simple: locate the landmine, then dismantle and remove it without causing an explosion. Simple, but very dangerous work. DEI work is often just as simple, and it can be just as dangerous too.

Fortunately, the threat of landmines is a problem I've never encountered firsthand here in the US, partly because this humanitarian crisis led to legislation banning their use. But there's still much work to be done on the ground to create a sense of safety. Even as I sit in my comfy office chair typing this sentence, I'm aware of the real need to comfort those healing from injuries caused by workplace landmines.

When my clients wrestle with fear of failure as they struggle to implement a DEI-related initiative, they often turn to something they feel they're good at, even if it's a nonsensical response. No matter how shiny someone's shoes are, spit-polishing an explosive device is not a useful response to the problem of landmines. Excellent polishing skills, a long history with the artform, or innovating some collaborative effort among the spit-polishers of the world won't help solve the problem either.

If I may go one step further, most DEI initiatives often start by plumbing the depths of the problem (think surveys and focus groups). Yet if the *source* of the problem is identified, it can be plucked out of the organization's environment and dealt with. To solve a problem, we don't need to know how the landmine was invented, who's responsible for its placement, or what the best polishing techniques are. Like landmines, DEI strategy needs to be approached from multiple angles simultaneously. Legislation, healing, disarmament, and military tactics—both offensive and defensive—must work together. And those angles don't involve

In the late 1980s, Princess Diana campaigned against the war practice of leaving explosives hidden across fields where innocent bystanders, animals, and vehicles could accidentally trip an explosion.

The solution was simple: locate the landmine, then dismantle and remove it without causing an explosion. Simple, but very dangerous work. DEI work is often just as simple, and it can be just as dangerous too.

shiny shoes. There's a time and a place for the skills we've learned, and when we perceive it isn't the time or the place, we fear failure.

When we ask questions, we usually expect answers. I invite us to allow the answers to seek the questions. What I mean by this is that sometimes our "answer" is just the first available option we're comfortable with, and it may not be appropriate or even applicable. I can't talk about our collective failure to make massive progress with DEI initiatives and not question whether we're focusing on the wrong elements. This reminds me of one of my favorite social justice quotes, reiterated to me by Francis E. Kendall on the front steps of a hotel in 2005: "Every system is exquisitely designed to produce the results that it gets."[1] Perhaps we're focusing too much on the fantasy of quick results and not enough on the systems designed to produce them.

Chuck couldn't digest all these unknown variables, and he just threw the opportunity into the trash can. This powerfully resourced leader who had the clearest intentions and best understanding was so close to doing something different. We were almost there.

At this edge, each of us has a choice: we can do something unknown, we can do the wrong thing again because it's safe and might eventually garner a different result, or we can do nothing. The response is up to you. The response is up to us.

We can do something unknown, we can do the wrong thing again because it's safe and might eventually garner a different result, or we can do nothing. The response is up to you. The response is up to us.

---

1   The origin of this quote is under debate. It's most commonly attributed to Dr. W. Edwards Deming, but Deming's original wording may have been altered and adopted by others, including Don Berwick and Dr. Paul Batalden.

Confused?

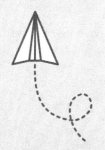

You, us, them, we, me — who is this book talking too? Chances are you have been delegated to read this book or participate in a discussion mastermind about this book from someone up the food chain a bit so I could be talking about "Them" — or others in your organization or even others in your industry. "Me" at times will mean you and I share a lot of my own stories so it could be me. "Us" could mean you and I or the small group of people that we are collaborating with. That brings us to we. "We" are all we got. Our them is their us and in our own us we show up. This does actually make sense — just may not be able to multi-task or speed read through this book.

You, us, them, we, me — who is this book talking to?

We are going on a trip that in itself is a disruption of what you are probably expecting out of a diversity business book. Getting comfortable with discomfort is being curious enough to find our own learning edges is progress. May that process never stop! What lies ahead is a pathway through our own organizational culture and mission in preparation for the next step. Instead of the next step flowing from the first, it is a stop gap between a habitual and conscious reaction where we can recognize where we get sidelined or derailed internally or externally. Once we recognize these patterns, we can do something about them in our responses.

There are a lot of unknowns on my part as to what this may mean for you, your us, y'all's them, and we are in this together. You will have to answer a lot of questions you likely don't know the answers to and more likely have never even been asked to answer before.

This is how to do the best you can with what you have some of the time because it is better than nothing never.

Let's keep going.

Follow the roadmap.

Let's Keep going.

Part Zero

Disrupting the Norm

Two comments I get frequently from my clients both involve "them":

1. What about *them*? *They* must do something different first.
2. *They* are always complaining about nonsense, and *they* just need to get back to work.

My response is to ask them these questions: "How is this line of thinking working out for you? How is waiting on 'them' or dismissing 'their' concerns serving you?"

It's time to do something different and disrupt our way of interacting with these folks. We need to act, and we need to listen. These two seemingly small things are revolutionary because they disrupt the culture we experience in our organizations. If we start doing something, others may follow. If we acknowledge that which we don't know or experience, others may feel heard. Regardless, we need to take action. We need to become the disrupters.

What has become normal for me is watching my highly resourced, powerful clients freeze between fear of being first (too vulnerable and risky) or being caught last at implementing diversity, equity, and inclusion (DEI), related. It seems to me that no one wants to go first. There also seems to be a shared pressure to not get caught too far behind the missing leader of the pack. This means that nothing happens while carrying the heavy load of missing the cues of perceived leadership in the DEI space.

This has become the new norm. It needs to be dismantled and I will settle for disrupted. There is no easy answer; best practices are not documented to lead the failure-free way forward.

We are in this together and we will need each other (even them) to guide a path forward together.

Ahead is a step-by-step process to assess what you have resource-wise, what you need to gather and share with others, as well as what you will need to listen and learn from outsiders to build something currently unknown.

Are you ready to disrupt?

Cut out this bookmark. No need to overthink it, wonder if you're the right person for the job, or go looking for scissors. Just give it a fold, hard crease it with your thumbnail, and rip.

TRYING TO MAKE SENSE OF THINGS?

Stop. This is part of the problem.

JUST KEEP READING.

pluralism

multiculturalism

tolerance

awareness

celebration

diversity

social justice

equality

equity

inclusion

belonging

justice

I don't care what
you call it, just
do something.

Fantastic. You are now a
disrupter. You didn't defer
the decision to another
person or to next week.
You didn't wait for it to
be perfectly measured.
You calculated your odds of
success and took action.

And now you're equipped
to flag a page you want
to come back to.

My clients fear going first
and feel confident that
they aren't in last place
so they do nothing... you
are doing something by
keeping doing something.

CHAPTER 1

Disruption

Disruption often comes in two forms, immediate and delayed, and we usually don't see either one coming. Back in 2003, I was living in Brooklyn when the Eastern Seaboard experienced a blackout. It hadn't dawned on me that my commute into Manhattan used electricity until I found myself walking home across the Brooklyn Bridge. By the time I got to my neighborhood, restaurants had lined up grills of all shapes and sizes along the sidewalks and were cooking meat before it spoiled. I imagined an all-hands-on-deck call going out to staff, with a plea to bring grilling supplies if they could make it into work.

The blackout was an immediate disruption, and it likely wasn't covered in any training or emergency preparation planning. People with cash bought dinner (many didn't expect change, knowing cash registers wouldn't be working), and everyone in my neighborhood acted like we knew each other. My block had suffered a lot of loss on 9/11, right before I moved to the city the following spring, and I'd heard about block parties and meal trains supporting families. On the first day of the power outage, I saw the whole block unite, support, and care for one another. Once the electricity returned, we all scurried back to our apartments. I won't forget this week, as it permanently disrupted the story I had about my neighborhood.

Disruption can also appear slowly, and we have to consciously take notice. Last night, my 15-year-old pug/lab, Leo, and I were getting ready for bed when I noticed how our bedtime routine has changed over time. He can't see or hear much these days (unless a single piece of grated cheese falls to the ground, but that's a different story!), yet I don't remember when that happened. I don't recall when having the step stool on my side of the bed became so normalized that now I instinctively know where it is and how to step over it without making noise when I let Leo out in the early morning hours. When did this start? My old dog has taught me a lot of new tricks. He still loves his couch time, sleeps in the same position on the bed, and does the dishes when the other dogs finish their food. And, it is true, this old man dog will likely never again run on the beach chasing sea foam or birds. Our routine has been disrupted, and I never even noticed.

I invite you to embrace disruption and normalize complexity whether you see it coming or not. Applying this practice to DEI initiatives may include responding to a crisis, hosting healing spaces, or facilitating conversations about how the knowns and unknowns are impacting each of us differently. The problem, concern, and outcome can all be disruptive to our expectations. By normalizing complexity, we can double down on the cultural experience inside of our organization and realign it — or disrupt it — for good.

I invite you to embrace disruption and normalize complexity whether you see it coming or not.

Efforts begun from a place of privilege in the name of advocacy or allyship often speak for or represent those who've been marginalized but do so without their consent, discussion, involvement, or collaboration. Each of our mistakes, missteps, failures, and *almost* successes are places of growth. Disruption isn't always terrible. Anything can be *almost* terrible while still being the right action, just like the right behaviors can unexpectedly land terribly on another. Disruption is growth. There is order in chaos, and changes can easily manifest into new, as-yet unimagined ways of being.

In 1953, after interviewing dozens of white-collar criminals, Sociologist, Dr. Donald R. Cressey, identified rationalization, pressure, and opportunity as the three elements required to commit fraud. Twenty years later, his model is widely known as **Cressey's Fraud Triangle**.

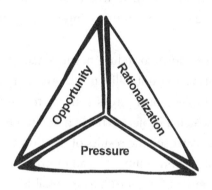

Cressey studied accounting crimes, fraud, corporate scandals, and organized crime and made significant contributions and concluded that an employee is led to commit fraudulent behaviors when all three elements are present. Over the years, refined definitions of these terms have included "capability," "coercion," "external regulations," "societal influences," and even "ignorance," "ego," "greed," and "arrogance." Possibly the biggest reason Cressey's Fraud Triangle is, to this day, a common element of accounting education, ethical certifications, and the like, is that it's used to show that to commit fraud, someone must have the opportunity or access to do the crime as well as potentially cover it up. Who better to embezzle money?... Wait... Don't answer that.

Even the most loyal employee who's otherwise of high moral character can be tempted to commit fraud and betray their employer's expectations. All it takes is rationalization, pressure, and opportunity. And if you're an accountant, all three are present all the time. An accountant can track where money comes from and goes to. Their job is to record this financial flow, and they're trusted with others' money. Being able to falsify records provides them with the ideal opportunity to commit fraud, but only if they have a motive, a personal incentive, or perhaps external pressure to do it paired with an attitude or rationalization for the crime itself. In the same situation, if there's a solid plan, pressure, and simultaneous motivation to do bad, some accountants will do bad things, and others may feel they have no choice but to blow a whistle out of a deep sense of integrity, or loyalty, not just to the organization, but to all of humanity. These behaviors can be justified when the right ingredients present themselves to go against the grain of preexisting expectations of an employee.

Companies make efforts to reduce negative factors that could lead to fraud by implementing accountability programs, increasing transparency expectations, and implementing cross-training to lessen risk. Some even design systems in which a project is broken down into such small pieces that team members can't see the results of their own work and therefore reducing a sense of responsibility. Instead of breaking things apart, why can't we build enticement for good? Isn't it possible that such enticement could be used for good too?

When someone is creating an initiative to increase employee morale or support the retention of existing talent, they too must go against current company culture. With time, talent, and resources, the opportunity alone might not be enough to do something, but it could spark an idea. Personal attitudes, motives, and rationalizations may shift and change as employees learn about the experiences of others, and they may want to step up as allies or advocates for acknowledgment, change, or a corporate stand on the subject. Perhaps other issues could be addressed that would also motivate or incentivize this employee to act for good. By recognizing societal pressures, current events, or internal pressures that are affecting us and our teams, we can bring these initiatives to the forefront.

Wanting to have all the details, answers, and specifics is also a motivation to act. Acting, as well as remaining inactive, stuck, or undecided, are responses in and of themselves. I posit that instead of using Cressey's model for identifying the risk of fraud or the likelihood of an employee committing harm, let's together use these same variables, rationalization, pressure, and opportunity for good. Either way, it disrupts the status quo.

Imagine if we could disrupt diversity initiatives and beyond simply by listening to the answers that are already presenting themselves, then asking questions that are new to us. Since we don't experience every problem that others face, others have answers to questions we haven't even imagined yet. Can we allow these answers to meet us where we are so that we can grow?

True disruption, however, can only be guided by generosity, curiosity, vulnerability, and authenticity. On one side, for example, consider Audre Lorde's speech and essay titled "The Master's Tools Will Never Dismantle the Master's House." On the other side, consider Albert Einstein's plea to wealthy Americans in 1946: "A new type of thinking is essential if mankind is to survive and move toward higher levels."[2] Lorde speaks to the pressure (or lack thereof) and unresponsive nature of those in power to act, and Einstein suggests that new answers from the outside must be sought for the current inside problems we've created.

Perhaps this is how Einstein imagined our consciousness levels shifting and changing so that we can use the tools we've grown accustomed to building new and begin dismantling the known structures that aren't serving us all. These variables lead not to illegal behavior but to disruption. Let's disrupt the status quo by creating opportunities to do good. That way, we can consciously act in a space between a reaction and an informed response.

By reframing Cressey's work from an illegal, immoral, fraudulent lens, to one that nurtures positive change, we can use these concepts

---

2   Albert Einstein, "Atomic Education Urged by Einstein: Scientist in Plea for $200,000 to Promote New Type of Essential Thinking," *New York Times*, May 25, 1946, nytimes.com/1946/06/23/archives/the-real-problem-is-in-the-hearts-of-men-professor-einstein-says-a.html.

of disruption to ask better questions and lead to better answers. DEI work is complex in its nature and needs to be continually reconsidered, redeveloped, and recreated. We need to normalize the complex nature of dismantling what is known to us and do the work anyway. Afterall, we have the tools that built, support, and maintain the very systems being disrupted. Using the tools we have to recharacterize our work could be the missing piece that would unlock progress. It seems worth a try.

What if we recharacterize Cressey's Fraud Triangle into something that allows the most resourced leaders in the organization to do the best they can with what they have some of the time? Using the same concepts and packaging them into DEI consulting language, we end up with something like this:

Cressey's Triangle	Do-Good Triangle	
rationalization		**prepare**
pressure *internal, external*		**recognize** *me, them*
opportunity		**respond**

If the complexity of DEI issues is accepted as normal, then this disruption framework can be used for good. First, let's look at this recharacterization as a disruption, then the importance of having all three variables deployed consciously at the same time as a roadmap to success.

What if we recharacterize Cressey's Fraud Triangle into something that allows the most resourced leaders in the organization (and world sometimes) to do the best they can with what they have some of the time?

Using the same concepts and packaging them into DEI consulting language, we end up with something like this:

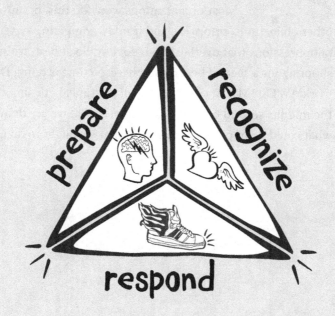

Remember, true success with regards to diversity, equity, inclusion, (DEI) work, is dismantle of all known systems and starting over to build something that is grounded in a sense of belonging and inclusion for all. Most organizations won't do this, because of other obligations, priorities, and frankly, competing systems of oppressions that overlay in our society. So at best, we are shooting for a second best option here. No one is doing DEI work AWESOMELY, consistently, all the time. Let's shoot for the middle, second best, at best, and see what we are doing well, what could be improved upon, and what we ought to do next.

CHAPTER 2

Normalizing Complexity

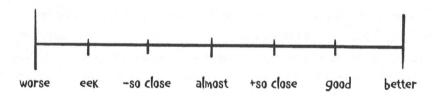

worse   eek   -so close   almost   +so close   good   better

If anything is both normal and complex for me as a DEI Consultant, it is that I both know and don't know the answers to the questions I prepare in advance and spontaneously ask. Reread this. It is confusing — unclear — and nonsensical — and that is just one example of a complicated situation that is actually a normal pattern. Often, I find my clients want a clean scale similar to this one, or even better, a list of exactly what to do in all circumstances to complete their DEI task at hand. No recipe here. My "job" is to illuminate the answers from within the organization — so technically — you, the reader, know them, I help you find them.

You may notice that "so close" is even listed twice, but I bet you know the difference. You can reflect on times when your actions missed the mark, almost right, and sometimes it was still pretty good, and others you were closer to making things worse. Only you know the difference between a negative or positive impact, and frankly, knowing or even noticing this difference is a practice that takes training. Focus on the learning from the choices you made, what you did do, and what you didn't, and keep working. Training is an on-going process and there is no known quick fix, best practice, or success story to follow.

Being "almost there" can become as motivating as the opportunity to get something right. The risk of an organization getting it "almost right" is never completing the work or cease trying to pick up the initiative again. A baby step that heads in the right direction but doesn't solve a problem can be harmful and at times it can be helpful. Even worse, it can become an excuse to never try again, even if it's the right thing to do. Every failed attempt at doing the right thing matters.

It's after deep reflection, therapy on my own, and a lot of ice cream that I've found the motivation in being almost there versus being so close and quitting. I don't want to be a part of someone giving up again, so I got to work on how to transform "- So Close" into a momentum building "almost," and I think I found it. Surprise! It's already happening as a regular business practice; it's just not yet rolled into your DEI plan. For me, the key was understanding the complexity of the issues facing my clients. This work is not linear, but cyclical.

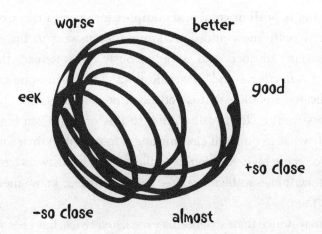

Almost Doing Good

Notice as a cycle instead of a linear model, worse and better are right next to each other. Worse for who? Change is threatening to many, and it takes someone to notice when things are actually getting better. We have to take notice (actively take notice) to assess where we are in any given moment. DEI work is not different.

It's astonishing to me that outside of a DEI context, we try new things all the time, yet when suggesting new initiatives under a DEI umbrella of sorts, we don't. No one wants to be first and fail nor be last due to a failure to respond earlier — so nothing happens. Outside of a DEI context, we invent things, try out new ideas, and build upon what others are doing, and sometimes, we simply do the best we can with what we have some of the time and go about our merry way. We also learn, adapt, and relearn all the time in our daily lives.

For example, the other day I had to parallel park on the left-hand side of a busy one-way street. I pride myself on being a great parallel parker. Once, I even parked a 24-foot U-Haul truck on a Saturday in Chinatown while helping a friend move in NYC (I should've gotten a medal for that one). I've identified as someone with a deep history of being able to park anything anywhere. Then I got a Fiat. At first I couldn't park that thing anywhere. The dimensions were so off. Yes, it could fit almost anywhere, but I was always sticking too far out of a space and never close enough to the curb. Rather than relearn, I just avoided parallel parking. Now I drive a hybrid, baby version of an SUV and feel like I should be way better at this; I feel like I'm learning something I once knew all over again.

There's nothing wrong with relearning, unlearning, noticing an avoidance, and learning again. So why can't we apply these reasonable and flexible skills of learning and unknowing to DEI initiatives? The short and most direct answer is that those with the most resources (finances, opportunity, authority, power, time, etc.) to dismantle the known power systems often don't have firsthand experience with oppression. Those most able also tend to feel threatened and defensive, are unaware of where to begin, or are under too much pressure to succeed. Enter the go-to, off-the-shelf solutions that label themselves "best practices." Instead, we could ask for help, process our own reactions, and work together to try for a better outcome with patience and curiosity.

Identifying that a need is present and alerting outsiders of a threat we don't understand and haven't experienced is doing the right thing at the right time even if it doesn't solve the problem or make the situation better. Almost is doing the right thing at the right time even if it doesn't work but leans toward a + so close, good, and not the other direction.

In my neighborhood a few weeks ago, a woman found a discarded artillery shell in her garden. She called the police who called in the bomb squad, and it was detonated on the beach for the public's safety.

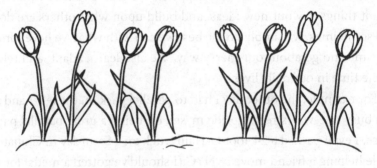

The gardener, who was likely not a ballistics
expert, called for help. Our local police force
also brought in help. It's likely that no one in my sleepy town ever knew we even had a bomb squad, let alone a detonation protocol. It was only when we heard a loud boom at 10 a.m. from the direction of the ocean that people started asking questions. The detonation protocol hadn't been used before because there was no need, yet there was preparation prior to a needed response. Back to gardening.

There's a lot to learn from this example. When we encounter an explosive device while knee-deep in tulip bulbs, it isn't the time to relish war stories or study up on best practices for disarming bombs. We need to defer to someone else, do our own part, and hope for the best — *almost*.

When we encounter an explosive
device while knee-deep in tulip
bulbs, it isn't the time to relish
war stories or study up on best
practices for disarming bombs.
We need to defer to someone
else, do our own part, and
hope for the best — <u>almost.</u>

What would you do if you found an errant artillery shell in your garden? Your reaction likely wouldn't follow a predetermined protocol, but it might sound something like, "HOLY SHIT! What is that?" Maybe you'd ask others to have a look and ask for their opinions, or you'd search the internet. At some point you'd know there's a problem and defer to others. The others may also have a holy-shit moment, but maybe they'd also have some knowledge of what to do. Meanwhile, you may be asking yourself questions like these:

- How did it get there?
- Is it dangerous?
- Is it better or worse to know I have a bomb in my garden?

Confession time! Seeing an armored vehicle roll down my tiny street while I was walking my dog was my own holy-shit moment. At any time, anything can go wrong, and even when we don't know what the wrong or right move might be, we often act anyway. We either use the resources we know about or pretend we saw nothing and change our gardening plans.

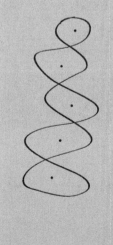

Often, best practices, consultant suggestions, and other tools are right in front of you in a report you haven't read that summarize patterns within your own organization through listening sessions, focus groups, surveys, assessment results, research. Even if you know of a problem beneath the surface, you may not face it until it becomes undeniable. Then you typically use the tools and resources you are used to using instead of asking for support because it is new, unknown, different, or just previously unconsidered.

DEI-related issues, initiatives, and social movements — even trying to articulate what all gets rolled into DEI work inside of an organization — is challenging. The commonality is the hard stuff we don't really know what to do with, about, or for. We can't even identify the right words.

As organizational leaders, we have the resources to solve social problems. Social problems "out there" impact every facet of an organization, including its stakeholders who are influenced by the creation, development, use, and disposal of an organization's product, service, or purpose. Everyone is impacted by the pain and suffering of being silenced, marginalized, oppressed, endangered, and ignored. Delegation practices, task forces, strategic plans, legislation, and wall murals aren't solutions. Each may serve a purpose in finding a solution, and each is better than doing nothing at all, but we must stop prettying up problems. We need to work toward identifying their sources rather than ignoring them because we aren't sure we'll be successful.

I see this pattern time and time again when working with organizational leaders. They ignore a known problem because there isn't a pre-established path forward. You can't unknow the problem, though it's very tempting to try. Latching onto a familiar "best practice" devolves into comfortably doing the wrong thing or never asking anything relevant to the problem at hand. There may be some transfer of skills and resources from our failed attempts at responding, and even

Stakeholder or Shareholder?

Instead of using the term shareholder, organizations need to broaden their target audience for accountability to not just shareholders, but those that are impacted from beginning to end, top to bottom, of an organization and its surrounding communities. Everyone has a stake in the world being better.

examples of successfully turning a blind eye can be utilized appropriately in different circumstances.

Spit-polishing a landmine is as dangerous as it is the wrong response, but it results in something pretty so we've gotten very good at it (see your organization's most recent annual report for an example). Making something pretty, or white/pink/green-washing marketing pieces that highlight only successes, inclusion or women, or sustainability contributions, is not entirely bad, but it often becomes a step in the wrong direction. Failed attempts in the right direction don't become wrong just because they didn't succeed. This is where "almost" comes in. The difference between "- So Close" and "Almost" matters a lot here. I was so frustrated with CEO Chuck when I pushed my chair back from his conference table because I felt that we were "+So Close" to really doing something revolutionary for his company. "+So Close" to almost doing good that could lead to something even better. "-So Close."

Feeling"-So Close" and their "EEK" is disappointing. I carried that feeling with me for years. Then, about a month ago, a group of colleagues and I were scheming and planning for a stay the following year in an Airbnb with spotty Wi-Fi and I got re-inspired. Inspiration came in the form of an Apple update. I noticed there was a new update on both my iPhone and my Mac. We were all Apple product people, so I asked if anyone had done the update yet to find out how big the file was, thinking that if it was large we'd need to plan how to share the unreliable Wi-Fi where we were meeting. One colleague casually mentioned that it "wasn't his turn yet." "Huh?" I asked. That's when I learned that not only do products get released that then require updates, but the updates themselves aren't released at the same time across the board. It's like how antenna-based televisions were slowly phased out as new technology evolved. My inspiration was about the slow roll out of updates so that any unexpected bugs or errors could be handled before the next wave of updates were announced. Outside of DEI initiatives, we already leave room for the unknown because we know it's likely to result in something we didn't think of. If only my clients could have the same sense of nimbleness when working on their DEI responses!

Spit-polishing a landmine is as dangerous as it is the wrong response, but it results in something pretty so we've gotten very good at it.

I was so frustrated with CEO Chuck
when I pushed my chair back from his
conference table because I felt that we
were "+So Close" to really doing something
revolutionary for his company. "+So Close"
to almost doing good that could lead to
something even better. "-So Close."

Feeling"-So Close" and their
"EEK" is disappointing.

Because I'm a diversity consultant, most of my work is at the intersection of expectations and constraints of different stakeholders. My clients often ask me to fix something or seemingly expect me to download best practices and make a problem go away. A "make it go away" approach cannot work. Leaders often ask comfortable or familiar questions rather than addressing actual concerns. One party asks for recognition and resolution to create something new, while another party reorganizes existing best practices just enough to look and feel busy but without much focus.

Our comfort levels may produce anticipated results, but that has gotten us to where we are today. If we challenge our comfortable, old, go-to moves, the result could be better responses and better outcomes.

As leaders, once we become aware of a problem we may not have firsthand experience with, we must focus on both our response system and the organizational design to get better results. By focusing on the intentional design of our organization — the structure itself — we can uncover the intention, focus, goal, ideal, and mission of our collective effort. If we ignore these elements, we're unable to generate new results, because the constraints on the questions provide space only for precise, previously known reactions.

These typical reactions are a challenge for those who have the time, context, and resources to do something differently but don't because the problem isn't one they've experienced themselves. After a bit of time, the same questioners circle back with what seem to be novel applications of new resources, but the same constraints that lead to ill-fitting reactions still exist.

Often when something is brand-new or hasn't been experienced, it doesn't make sense. Normalizing complexity and trusting each other to take a leap into the unknown is how we will shift from quietly planning to actively leading the way, from an entitlement of knowing to the vast potential of curiosity. There's a new way of thinking about DEI initiatives that achieves this by normalizing the complexity of the pain and suffering occurring in your organization, and it encompasses five assumptions:

Normalizing complexity and trusting each other to take a leap into the unknown is how we will shift from quietly planning to actively leading the way, from an entitlement of knowing to the vast potential of curiosity.

- At best, you're already doing the second-best thing — as no one is doing the best thing.
- It's never the wrong time to do the right thing even if it doesn't work.
- Do the best you can with what you have some of the time because it's better than doing nothing all the time.
- No one else is going to do it for you.
- Follow or lead. PS — No one is leading yet.

No matter the funding, experience, interest, habit, reputation, or dedication, every organization I work with has tried something that never got off the ground. Their efforts have failed, trailed off, lost steam, been forgotten, or didn't wildly succeed. By normalizing the complexity, we can see that DEI initiatives are no different.

check-in

ME TOO! I look around this intersection of comfort and fear, waiting for more questions to be asked. I hear none, and yet I feel like different options are screaming out, asking to be tried. Perhaps I was bursting to write this book because I'm an answer collector searching for the right questioner. I see people trying and getting close, then either checking a box of completion or calling it a failure while one lone wolf keeps trying.

CHAPTER 3

Follow the Do-Good Triangle

There's a pattern of threes that, in itself is an example of order. Humor writers highlight jokes that come in sets of three, and chaos theory is often represented by a triangle pattern often called a "three-winged bird" of chaos when random behaviors are tracked over time. In my first book, *Good Enough Now*, I too used a three pronged model, of Head (details), Heart (ideas), and Action (paralysis or doing), that overlays nicely with Cressey's triangle. The key in the power of three isn't that there are three independent variables that complete a whole, but that the three elements are dependent on one another.

The best example of the power of three elements is the 1984 version of *Ghostbusters* when the three main characters defeat the demigod Zuul by crossing the streams of their three proton packs. The Ghostbusters had assumed that crossing the streams would be dangerous and therefore never tried it, but they took a risk, and it paid off. (Perhaps I should've given a SPOILER ALERT.)

Disrupting the status quo with your DEI initiatives begins by 1) taking advantage of listening, 2) recognizing something we're not experiencing firsthand, and 3) responding by doing better. I can't think of anything more disruptive than lasting change for good!

The key in the power of three isn't that there are three independent variables that complete a whole, but that the three elements are dependent on one another.

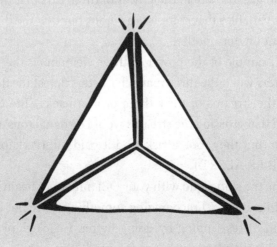

Before we can successfully disrupt for good by following the Do-Good Triangle, we must do our own organization's work and often this shows up utilizing one maybe two of the elements Prepare, Recognize, and Respond. Each are important and can be utilized in any order, even repeated. You may even notice different attempts at DEI work in each element, and it isn't until all three are brought together can these efforts truly disrupt the status quo and build something better. We must do so by curiously and vulnerably noticing and authentically moving into action to inspire others to follow our lead. When enacted fully, the Do-Good Triangle will incorporate your individual, organizational, and industry's resources, to increase a sense of belonging in the world.

check-in

I'm confused. Huh?

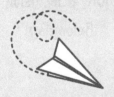

Three elements need to be used together on three levels at the same time, in any order, over and over again. Similar to the shift from thinking of just shareholders, we are expanding to think of everyone, all stakeholders, that are impacted in anyway from our organization's existence. Only when we take responsibility for ourself, workplace, and community, can our resources be put to the best and most powerful work. The concept of corporate social responsibility looks for social problems that can be resolved through corporate resources that align with the organization's realm of influence, and are relevant to the industry. This expansion of thought examines every step of a widget's development, from natural resources to development to shipping to market to user to disposal, or across the value chain. If we are normalizing complexity and looking to disrupt for good, we must keep all of these elements linked together to have the most powerful impact.

What is better than a pattern of 3?
How about 3 sets of three things
that all happen at once? The Do-Good
Triangle model is about disruption for
good and like other DEI initiatives, you
can begin the work on multiple fronts
as long as you are doing the work.

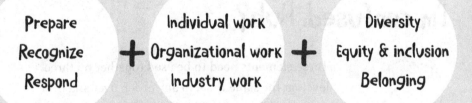

Prepare
Recognize
Respond

+

Individual work
Organizational work
Industry work

+

Diversity
Equity & inclusion
Belonging

Like a tandem bicycle - each rider is pedaling and
together they build momentum in the same direction.

1. First Variable: Prepare

To prepare means taking responsibility for your own lived experiences, for who and how you show up, and for the stories you write about others. If this is too much to ask, then determine why your organization matters. What is your organization's culture? What is inside your scope of responsibility? Outside of scope? Who are your key stakeholders? How does being a part of your organization show up for those across your value chain? Knowing how your organization's style, artifacts, norms and customs, language, beliefs, and values are or are not in alignment with your organization's mission is all the preparation you need to make personal, organizational, and industry changes.

2. Second Variable: Recognize

To recognize means asking yourself how you're serving as a role model to elevate your industry's standards. Do your own internal work (personal or organizational) to pave the way for others by transparently sharing your failed attempts at doing good. Recognize that others are complicated and have survived a lot to be present with you and therefore are worthy of the benefit of the doubt. The pressure you feel is your responsibility, as is the pressure your organization puts on others. Holding space for both internal and external evaluation will expand our impact and inspire others to do the same. We must first uncover what holds us back and what there is to gain from outsiders.

> **Recognize that others are complicated and have survived a lot to be present with you and therefore are worthy of the benefit of the doubt.**

Holding space for both internal and external evaluation will expand our impact and inspire others to do the same.

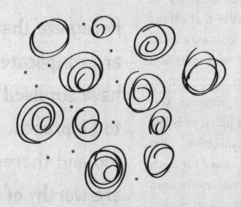

3. Third Variable: Respond

To respond is claiming the opportunity to do something that aligns with your organization's mission but disrupts your industry and encourages your stakeholders to do the same. Get on board with all that you have access to — the good, the bad, and the ugly — and do the best you can with what you have some of the time. You can do good, motivated by knowing your initiatives will inspire others to do the same.

Most of my clients' failed attempts to do good through their DEI initiatives begin with only one or two of these important elements. Intentionally developing a cyclical habit of using all three variables and generously modeling the way for stakeholders and industry partners is entirely different, and it could be just the disruption we're looking for. Doing so also grants permission for other industry partners, community members, and co-workers, to try without the risk of being shamed for failing. The key here is to be prepared, then build the ability to recognize and respond to problems you may not even experience but have the resources to disrupt.

check-in

Remember this is Part Zero! If you are trying to make sense of all of this now — STOP — I am just laying the groundwork of where we are going. Honestly, trying to make sense of everything is likely causing you more problems anyway so stop and trust the process. It is right there on the front cover that this is not a model of explicit answers, only questions, so let's get started. Take a second and ask yourself these questions. Bonus points will be given if you ask them as an individual, your organization, and as your industry. What if the worst happens? What if you can learn from others' missteps? What if you consciously choose to do good with the resources, power, vision, and perspective you know you have? What if it worked?

We must consciously create more vulnerable, curious, generous, and authentic, moments with and for each other so that we can do good and role model for others how to do the same. I often need to remind myself and others of our sense of urgency and that we are in control of ourselves. If we can remember this, perhaps the right opportunity will appear when we have all three variables, Prepare, Recognize, Respond, ready so that our doing good can last. Our mindsets may shift and change as we learn about the experiences of others, but if all three variables that make up the Do-Good Triangle are accessible, it's likely that someone will try to do something good that betters the whole.

What if the worst happens?

What if you can learn from others' missteps?

What if you consciously choose to do good with the resources, power, vision, and perspective you know you have?

What if it worked?

First Variable: Prepare

Learning from past missteps or mistakes is a great learning foundation. It's from our past answers, choices, reactions, and responses that we can ask more questions that better prepare us to do good. Easy enough. But is it?

My maternal grandfather, "Papa," as I remember him, was frugal, cautious, and risk averse. He was an accounting professor who carefully saved money until later in life. Even with all his life experience, he fell victim to multiple pyramid schemes that disrupted his entire way of living. He got entangled and ended up losing his entire savings, and he filed for bankruptcy before his passing. Preparation, lived experience, and rational decision-making can fall prey to a change in motive or attitude in the blink of an eye. Papa justified all his decisions while we cleaned out his garage full of bulk-purchased trucker hats, ball-point pens, and other items that drained his life savings away. Trust me, we are asking the same question to this day. Why would his behaviors change so drastically? Did he recognize these changes? We don't know. As stark of a contrast this is, it also showcases that disruptions happen and complications are normalized and this reality needs to be safe guarded against so that the mission of your organization can do the best work industry wide while you can also still look yourself in the mirror.

Having clarity in our reasoning doesn't always mean we're making the best choices, even if they feel right at the time. At the root of all rationalization is the balance between self-interest and public interest, or individualism and collective responsibility. Who do you feel responsible for, and how do you use your own agency to conduct yourself accordingly? Some feel responsible for themselves or their immediate family, others may expand their circle to include their neighbors, and some feel responsible for seven generations ahead. Understanding our own scale of responsibility can assist with the minutia of details and what we choose to do with them.

Why do whistleblowers, allies, advocates, and accomplices act as if they have no other choice than to do good, while others are compelled to commit and attempt to justify crimes? Because even when we have a clear mission that guides our choices, preparation isn't enough on its own. We need to pair this preparatory work with the other elements to be truly in our power. A good place to start is looking at our own attitudes and how we rationalize our actions. (Don't forget you are doing this work individually, organizationally, and industry wide!) In our handling and not handling of DEI initiatives, responses, or even knee-jerk reactions, *we* are responsible for who and how we are in the world. Where motive, incentive, and rationalization may be the "heady" parts of our do-good choices, they're only a few components of what's needed to successfully disrupt our existing workplace cultures and elevate our industries' standards.

Second Variable: Recognize

A lot of DEI initiatives fail because they're being developed or implemented from only one side of the Do-Good Triangle, and that's not enough. No room for failure means no innovation.

Buckling to internal and external pressures may make sense politically or even financially. However, trying matters, even when it's exhausting, and we're trying to disrupt for the good of our stakeholders, communities, and industries. Ideally, instead of succumbing to inbound pressures that lead to misguided reactions, we can learn to recognize these pressures for what they are and develop initiatives that serve the voices we learn to listen to.

Imagine the harm that's done at the hands of poorly planned initiatives that were quick fixes. Compare that to the ability to apply pressure on other organizations to elevate their work while we're disrupting our current way of doing business so that all voices are heard while also being in alignment with our beliefs and/or values. Often though, we recognize a problem, but aren't sure what we think of feel about it because we haven't done that preparatory work. Sometimes not launching something does less harm, and at times doing nothing lowers expectations, creating an atmosphere that is our current workforce experience. Keeping our heads down for the sake of profits is what we're aiming to disrupt. Launching into action without recognition won't last without recognizing real concerns existing around us. Imagine deciding food insecurity is a problem your organization wants to address and hasn't understood that food insecurity impacts your staff not just those abroad. Moreover, the actions decided to be taken may not be in agreement with the promises you have made to your stakeholders.

The very premise to do good and inspire others to do the same is the idea behind disruption for good. We must build up the skills to be able to recognize problems we may not experience firsthand but have the resources to solve. For instance, Executive Order 13769 was President Donald Trump's "Muslim travel ban" that he enacted on immigrants of a certain faith and ethnicity between January and March of 2017. In my zeal to advocate against this injustice and show solidarity with my friends, I posted a trending hashtag on my social media feed: "Until this ends, I am Muslim." Huzzah!

Within days, I'd lost three friends. Two of them identified as Muslim and were deeply offended. The other was disappointed that I would appropriate a cultural or religious identity in such a matter-of-fact manner and without empathy for the plight of religiously marginalized people. What did I really know about being Muslim, and how could I advocate for them without being educated on or having a real understanding of their culture? These are valid questions.

My motivation may have been in the right place, and I had an understanding of how social media algorithms work in getting messages seen by others, but this wasn't enough. Though my intentions were good, I caused real pain and experienced real loss because I wasn't thinking about the impact my post would have on others. I had the right idea and lacked self awareness that could have better informed my actions.

I have a lifetime membership in one of the more privileged clubs: White, temporarily able-bodied, educated, upper-class, cisgender, American woman. Nothing I do will take that membership away from me. I work hard to advocate for and educate on behalf of members of one of the more misunderstood and often marginalized communities: the LGBTQ+ community. I've spent years rooting out those misunderstandings and finding ways to bridge the knowledge gap between our lack of understanding and our genuine desire to be better, because I really believe we all want to be and do better every day. Though my social media pronouncement did resonate with many people, and although not all the feedback I received was negative, losing three friends hurt. Yet it forced me to think more carefully about my engagement in society and my perceptions of identity.

So, just who do you think you are? Nobody knows you better than you. Full stop.

We are all better off once we set aside our need to impose our biases and beliefs on others and instead ask, "How can I do better at seeing you the way you see yourself?" To be an ally in the world is to trust that someone knows themself better than you know them. I'm not a psychologist, but I have seen, heard, and learned enough to know that if someone has found a home in their identity, I will celebrate and validate it. We all deserve to feel at home. The idea of "home" applies on the individual, organizational, and industry level because self-awareness and recognition ought to go hand in hand. Sometimes we leap without doing all of this prep work when we see a problem. For this disruption for good to stick, we need to consciously employ and deploy all three variables at once.

We are all better off once we set aside our need to impose our biases and beliefs on others and instead ask, "How can I do better at seeing you the way you see yourself?" To be an ally in the world is to trust that someone knows themself better than you know them.

Third Variable: Respond

Just do something!!! Doing nothing is also a something, so how do you decide what to do or not do? Taking action is part of the circular cycle of diversity programming itself, so an initiative is bound to fail if we act on one variable of the Do-Good Triangle without addressing the other two. Even with a solid plan and great urgency, an initiative will only get *so close* if it isn't deployed with adequate support, assessment, and nimbleness to persist. It's in this moment that we get to decide whether we're going to do something and whether that something is for good or for bad. The woman who decided to put a daisy in the barrel of a rifle as a sign of peaceful protest against the Vietnam War did something for good. The parents who are turning in their guns to protect their children from accidents, as well as those who are taking gun safety classes and keeping weapons in their homes to protect their family's property, are also choosing to do good. Each is also an example of different areas or scopes of focus, international politics and war, security and home defense, and individual responsibility. I am drawing this parallel on purpose because we have to be acting on all three levels — individual, organization, and industry to truly disrupt for good.

In all cases, there's an opportunity to do good, and that good can be designed to benefit stakeholders and beyond. The Montgomery bus boycott is a prime example. After many failed attempts to get national attention, the NAACP and a local community organizer partnered together for the right opportunity that would garner media attention to the injustice of segregation. The plan was rehearsed, practiced, and implemented, but the perfect opportunity lay in wait. On December 5, 1955, while Rosa Parks was seated in the first row of the "colored section" of the bus, the deputized bus driver demanded that she stand to allow a White passenger to sit in her row. She refused to move and was arrested, though she wasn't breaking the law. Because of Parks' popularity and community support around Alabama, the incident drew statewide attention. Soon, the audacity of segregation practices that had created a cultural norm of prioritizing White passenger comfort expanded to a real understanding across the country: the ludicrous motivation of systemic racism. Mind you, systemic racism did and still does exist across our country, but the trifecta of intense societal pressure rising after a local community hero was arrested for not breaking the letter of the law elevated the opportunity to apply pressure on the entire country to eradicate segregation practices. This illuminated the racist motivations of segregation laws, which led to a 381-day bus boycott and, eventually, federal desegregation legislation.

Sixty years later, a Black woman named Bree Newsome and a White man named James Ian Tyson met for the first time over breakfast to confirm the details for the day's activism before walking to the capitol building in Columbia, South Carolina. Shortly after a mass shooting at Emanuel African Methodist Episcopal Church in Charleston, Newsome and Tyson had decided to remove the Confederate flag from capitol grounds. Newsome climbed the flagpole and began removing the flag while Tyson stood close by. When local police arrived on the scene, they were contemplating using their tasers on the metal pole to get Newsome down. Tyson reacted by placing his White hand on the pole, thinking that the police would be less likely to electrocute him than a young Black woman disobeying orders. Sadly, he was right. The police immediately put their tasers away and eventually took both activists into custody. While Newsome had removed the flag, Tyson had saved her life.

Take a moment to identify times when you've reacted or responded like any of the players that day in South Carolina:

- When have you taken action, such as climbing the flagpole?
- When have you done little things or made small gestures that have big impacts, such as putting your hand on the flagpole?
- When have you thought about taking action without thinking it all the way through?

Those police officers may not have initially thought of using their tasers, yet after they did, they changed their minds when they recognized

Sixty years after Rosa Parks refused to give up her seat on a bus, a Black woman named Bree Newsome and a White man named James Ian Tyson met for the first time over breakfast to confirm the details for the day's activism before walking to the capitol building in Columbia, South Carolina.

Later that day, to stop Bree Newsome from being tasered by police during their peaceful action, Tyson would place his White hand on a flagpole, thinking the police would be less likely to electrocute him than a young Black woman disobeying orders. Sadly, he was right.

that it may have harmed both Tyson and Newsome. Likewise, we can choose to either change our minds or proceed within the gap between reaction and conscious response. If we choose to stay in the gap, intervention, advocacy, allyship, and other initiatives may stall out before they get started, leaving folks behind along with all the complications. Let's break down how.

In order to act, we must first have a firm understanding of how we act, when we act, and when we do not. Paralysis is an action- or inaction-based reaction. To interrupt a situation, we must take several aspects into consideration, including our individual histories. We need to recognize whether we feel safe and prepared enough to not be just a bystander. If not, then acting in person may not be best. Perhaps instead, making a phone call, bearing witness, or recording what's occurring can help the situation while also keeping us feeling safe.

Please note that there's a significant difference between discomfort and lack of safety. Any act of intervention can lead to real lived experiences and change, both for the individuals involved and potentially on an even larger scale. Bias, both positive and negative, can lead to prejudice, which can develop into hatred and acts of violence. These acts do not have to be criminal to be powerful, just like our acts of trying do not have to be lethal to be effective. Trying again next time means we must be curious enough to reflect on what has happened, generous enough to assume that we could make a difference by doing good, and prepared enough to fail. Failure is the best teacher, and it fuels our practice of role modeling vulnerability and authenticity for others.

Trying matters. When in doubt, trying to try is the first step. It's also true that trying can be exhausting. Trying can be trying. But when combining our preparation, recognition, and response practices, trying is often all we can do. When we try, we must be clear in our intentions, then monitor, develop, adjust, and take responsibility for them so we can do better next time. And we must do so while showcasing for others how we're responding from our aligned culture. This is the only way to generously influence others to do the same.

Trying also means making room for failure and sharing that failure with others. Few in senior leadership positions celebrate failure, let alone tell others about it. I think this is an easy place to start.

While being disruptive, failing, and being a role model across your industry, you may face backlash, negative publicity, and possibly a loss in profits, but you will know why. Knowing the *why* behind your disruption is how change will stick. Change will last because your choices are rooted in your mission. Instead of succumbing to pressures, you can apply pressure to others to follow suit, and together we can do something radically different to benefit us all. By doing something different and allowing our answers to seek more questions, we all benefit. As when polishing stones, we must go against the grain of what's known to create something new. Then and only then can we elevate others to do good — and shine.

> Trying means making room for failure and sharing that failure with others. Few in senior leadership positions celebrate failure, let alone tell others about it. I think this is an easy place to start.

Knowing who we are and how we show up is an ongoing process that allows us to try. The act of trying depends on a conscious act of connection, both with ourselves and with others. Bear in mind that perfection is not the goal. For any change to occur, we must do something radically different than merely expecting the same actions to render new outcomes. Waiting around for others to perform the heavy lifting does not work. The onus lies with each of us taking responsibility for our own lived experiences and understanding how these crucible opportunities both impair and motivate our desire to connect and communicate with each other. This is the radical action needed to consciously foster innovative, thriving, and inclusive communities through all our lived experiences — good, bad, ugly, or awesome. Organizationally, the same applies.

Trying is about doing something regardless of fear, insecurity, trepidation, or worry about failed previous experiences. Accepting and constantly seeking failure allows us to try with equal excitement, time and time again. Remember, being "Good Enough Now" is about doing the best you can with what you have some of the time.

Once we check our rationalization or the pressure being applied to do something (or not), trying is the next step. "But ... but ...," some of you might be saying in an attempt to justify not knowing what to do or when to do it. We're talking about trying to try because it's the right thing to do. A good attitude or strong rational argument isn't always enough. If we can cross the streams of the Do-Good Triangle, we can disrupt for good.

We'll begin with preparation, then build up recognition skills and develop our response practices. As we cover these three areas, different processes and questions may arise within you. I suggest you take note of all the answers that appear before you and see whether they need to seek more questions. Think of this book as a cultural transformation manual and me as a thought partner or friend guiding you through a review of costly failures that were meaningful steps in the right direction. Plus, I'll give you some tough love, humor, and a lot of side-eye.

This is your warning to buckle up. Whether you're ahead of the game, caught up in it, or looking to be a role model for your industry, we can use disruption for good together.

check-in

Take a minute and take notes of all of the things you are good at — now. What was it like at the beginning? No one wants to eat my first loaf of bread or play me at ping pong. I am still very bad at both but I got a little better. I never saw any improvement in golf, and I am pretty sure there is still a police order in the state of Florida at one putt-putt location where I am banned for life. People in sales are told to constantly seek rejection because it is one step closer to a sale. Comedians aim to bomb to learn in real-time. What have you tried? What have you learned? What have you unlearned? What have you gotten good at? What are you good at that you still need to practice staying good?

Almost Doing Good

Part 1

Prepare

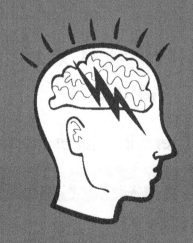

Part 1: Prepare

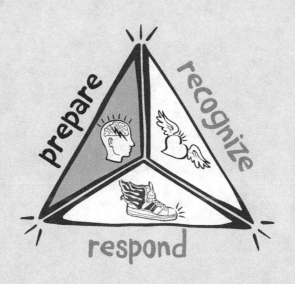

prepare

recognize

respond

What if X happens?

Hey! There is a landmine here!

typical response ~~I don't see one.~~

better response

Hey, team, we don't stand for landmines.

This is what we're doing. Any updates? Suggestions? Are we missing the mark anywhere? What can we do to support others?

"Increase diversity by 13.8 percent." I see goals of this kind or something similar quite often in strategic plans, and they're a dead giveaway that there hasn't been enough preparation work completed. It's possible that such goals are responses to something leaders recognize as an issue, but preparation is needed for measurement, progress, and success.

To adequately prepare, an organization must understand its own culture. That's the only way its leaders can define what "diversity" means in the first place, let alone know how a 13.8 percent increase could happen, by when, and from what starting point. What does 13.8 percent even mean if leaders don't know what currently exists? The disruption needed here is clarity, introspection, and defined guidelines of what is and is not part of the organization's culture.

The best preparation for an organization doesn't start with identifying the X in the question, "What if X happens?" That would be a step backward. Identifying all the possible versions of X is a great way to spend a consultant's time, but I'm actually trying to help solve their problems by asking questions like these:

- Why would it matter in the first place whether X happens?
- How would X challenge, affirm, support, or disrupt what the organization's leaders think they already know?

This is a preparatory question process that identifies the culture of an organization, from which all decisions are made, supported, adjusted, dismantled, and monitored. If you prefer, you can answer these questions for yourself:

- What is the culture of being with, in, around, and through your organization?
- What do you not even know you don't know about your own team? Your office? The industry? The surrounding community?

To prepare means to understand the nitty gritty of your organization and take full responsibility for what you determine is within your own scope of agency. This is one element of the Do-Good Triangle, and it's required to truly disrupt the systems we often navigate without even noticing their consequences.

I'm not a therapist, but I have been in therapy for more than 40 years. When individual work is assigned, it's often referred to as internal "self-work." This may be tracking down your inner child, rediscovering when you found your own sense of agency, or anchoring the moment(s) you decided who and how you want to be in the world. To be prepared for whatever's coming your way, you must become competent with various tools and have them ready when needed. Organizational work is no different.

Here are some starter questions for you to reflect on and share with your leadership team. SPOILER ALERT: if you don't have immediate and consistent answers, there's work to be done:

- What are the beliefs and values of your organization?
- How are you using language to align with these principles?
- When reviewing policies, practices, and traditions, is there something that can bolster your mission across your industry?
- At each point of contact, can you intentionally align this mission online, in hand, visually, and throughout each part of the stakeholder experience?

Bonus question

If you tapped into the social hubs, community influencers, and strong personalities in your organization, would they align with your leadership's answers? If not, open communication and work together to establish a congruent culture.

Let me guide you through these much-needed conversations so that you can use the skills you already have to give yourself some grace, inspire others, and elevate your industry.

Prepare to prepare.

CHAPTER 4

Identify Organizational Culture

Being prepared is a skill that must be rehearsed, practiced, and always kept within hand's reach. To do so is to grow comfortable with not knowing something, energized by the curiosity to find out and humble enough to be very publicly wrong, all while doing the right thing anyway. Knowing what the right thing is depends on a clear understanding of your organization's culture.

Culture is an appropriate starting place when preparing for the unknown, but I want to take a step back for a second. To think you know your organizational culture is to already make a big assumption. If you're a founding leader, you most likely knew what your organization's culture was like when you started. Perhaps you lost touch with reality as the organization grew, and you became increasingly more protected, sheltered, and screened. You may no longer have any idea what it's like to work for or with your own organization.

Organizational culture is a familiar concept but one that's hard to put our finger on. Take different circles of friends as an example. There are unwritten rules of who and how to be in a particular group as well as how that group interacts with their surroundings. It's similar with individuals. As a funny person, for instance, I often tell people that I can't be offended. Although this is generally true, I'm also a sensitive person who *can* take offense. Groups of friends of mine often use humor in very different ways, which is why a mixed-company road trip, dinner party, or Zoom gathering may cause some anxiety among us — our unspoken rules may clash with one another as our cultures mix and match.

We often do or don't do something because it's what we're used to doing or not doing to adhere to our unspoken values. When I first moved in with my partner, Loren, I had to learn to never pick up any jar by its top because the lid was likely not screwed down. We're now almost 20 years in, and I still don't get this one. Honestly, he doesn't either; he just doesn't really screw lids back on. It's not in a manual (trust me, I checked), yet I quickly learned not to cry over spilled pickles.

So, I ask you this:

- What lids aren't screwed on under your leadership?
- Does everyone know and accept this risk?
- Do you know how your desired culture is experienced by your stakeholders?
- Do you know how *you* are experiencing it?
- If you don't know your organization's culture, who does?

These are not easy questions to answer, but they are crucial questions to ask. And it should be obvious that no one else can answer them for you. It's those who live these experiences every day, at each point of contact, who can.

You first have to know what you want your organizational culture to be in order to see whether you're fostering it accurately. A small startup founded in New Zealand by four college friends, for example, experiences a very different organizational culture than a 10-year-old company consisting of 80,000 employees across 11 countries. This same

To prepare means
to understand the
nitty gritty of your
organization and take full
responsibility for what
you determine is within
your own scope of agency.

start up is now 10 years old and there's a different level of investment, aspiration, and commitment, not to mention burnout, obligation, and enforced rigidity.

An organization's nimbleness is directly related to a solid understanding of the way each moving part works, both simultaneously and autonomously. The number of CEOs who tell me in exasperated voices that they "wish people would just be straight with them" is astounding. It's also surprising because these are the same people who have five-minute stand-up meetings with their direct reports, delegating underlings to prioritize exactly what they can and cannot attend to. What these leaders long for are the high-risk and stressful build-up days when their successes and failures were at their own fingertips. At that time, they couldn't even imagine how growth would skew their perspectives, stifle the flow of information, and leave them in the dark. Preparation matters and is never-ending.

A tech company that grew out of a garage into a global empire might have members with similar values or beliefs to those they had the moment they sparked the company into existence, but they should ask themselves these questions:

- Has the company changed at all since it was created?
- If it's changed in the country of origin, what about other locations?
- What other revenue streams have developed over the years?
- Does each employee today believe the same things the founders did?
- For that matter, do the founders believe in the same things today that they did back then?

It seems impossible — I'll hedge my bets and say it's at least unlikely — that founding documents, values, and beliefs would be accurate across the board forever and always. Do not tell me what the founding documents say. You probably can't find them, anyway, nor have you read them. If given that task, you'd likely be tempted to delegate it. Besides, the surrounding content, industry, and world have changed, rendering these precious documents obsolete or even irrelevant today, right?

What if you're wrong? What if these founding documents actively inform all decisions at all levels around the world? In that world, we might be better prepared to respond to the unexpected, to unknowns we don't know about yet or can't even imagine.

Most failed DEI initiatives start with the term "culture" but without much grasp of what that term even means. Your organization's culture, like riding a tandem bicycle, means knowing your organizational style, company artifacts, typical norms and customs, and language and how they align (or don't) with your foundational beliefs and values. Once in alignment, like multiple riders pedaling together, momentum can build to support any new initiative leading to sustained success.

Even with the best onboarding processes, there are little things that don't make it into the curriculum yet are experienced at work. Let me break down what you're looking for to identify the culture of your organization:

1. Organizational Style

In a typical corporate working environment, the objective is to recruit, hire, and train talented people with specific skills that are used for profit. This is already a strange arrangement. Looking at each point of contact with different stakeholders can show how power is shared (or not), how information is shared (or not), who answers questions that are asked, and even who gets to ask questions. This is all part of your organizational style.

2. Artifacts

There are objects, items, or things, so to speak, that are known by insiders (or at least some of them) and are just normal parts of a group's culture. For example, one company allows employees to wear comfortable, sleeveless, fleece vests while another expects their employees to wear name tags and uniforms. Some hospitals assign different colors of scrubs for different kinds of healthcare workers, while others don't require scrubs at all. Some employees have their own offices with doors and windows, and others share a space with multiple people on different shifts. These things matter and have a significant impact on the culture of your organization.

3. Norms & Customs

The culture of any group isn't always documented well (or at all), and it often isn't acknowledged until a norm or custom is violated. Policing dress codes, wording, or tone may be emphasized as strongly as not tolerating arriving to or staying at work late, and picking up extra tasks, or participating in team-building exercises is often referred to as "mandatory fun." Concepts such as professionalism, decorum, or even hygienic expectations are often not explained or documented, but employees need to learn them if they're going to successfully navigate the organization's culture.

4. Language

Like strutting peacocks, we use certain words or internal jargon to show our position in a group. But we have to change gears in mixed or outside settings. Our language can bind us, but it can also serve as a gatekeeper or ostracize others. Sometimes these "secret insider languages" are industry-specific, and they often show up as inside jokes, references, or project-specific terms that are experienced inside and/or outside an organization's culture.

5. Beliefs & Values

Knowing the "why," or aligning with the vision and mission of an organization, can be as subjective as being "fit" for an organization's culture. This can be a performance, or it can be genuine, but to define a purpose and stay in alignment with it is an essential element of all organizational decisions.

Most failed DEI initiatives start with the term "culture" but without much grasp of what that term even means. Your organization's culture, like riding a tandem bicycle, means knowing your organizational style, company artifacts, typical norms and customs, and language and how they align (or don't) with your foundational beliefs and values. Once in alignment, like multiple riders pedaling together, momentum can build to support any new initiative leading to sustained success.

Who's taking the time to teach, explain, or demonstrate these realities? Almost no one. Because we often don't acknowledge that we even know this information. We don't know what we know, and we don't know what we don't know. So let's begin by preparing in advance and keeping this process open and available for all to utilize, reference, repeat, and improve.

The fear that I'm most often challenged to help subside is a fear of a known happening but with an unknown consequence. I once posted on LinkedIn and Facebook that I was working on something new and asked followers to comment, in any context, what their biggest fear was, as in "What if X happens?" Some people listed their fears regarding illness, disability, death, being cared for, caring for those they leave behind, being rejected, or ending up unsuccessful. Others listed more optimistic fears, such as not being able to inspire enough joy or curiosity in others, having their children not need them anymore, and being closer to success than they imagined. Some commented that their biggest fears were about politics, environmental impacts, and access to water, peace, justice, and the like. One friend from graduate school commented, "Not sure if this is helpful, but I can't read this right now. Too much stress, too many questions I'm not prepared to ask. Good on you for diving into this space. I cannot."

The fears that were listed are largely out of our control and not directly related to our own behaviors or responsibilities. Thus, the "it" in "What if it happens?" is often out of our control, hence the fear. When it comes to DEI initiatives, there are often more knowns than unknowns, yet we're still fearful.

I think we're better prepared to discuss the unknown than we are to grapple with what we do know and what we know we don't know. Even when discussing our fears, we'd benefit from asking more questions. So now I ask you this: What would you have to do to be prepared to ask more questions? Is there something you can do with the power, resources, time, energy, inclination, and ability you have? Can you use them to not only benefit the bottom line of your organization but also

The "it" in "What if it happens?"
is often out of our control,
hence the fear. When it comes
to DEI initiatives, there are often
more knowns than unknowns,
yet we're still fearful.

make you and everyone involved throughout the entire value chain feel more considered, heard, and included?

Let's dive into preparation and address head-on both the known and unknown fears regarding what DEI initiatives may mean or look like for you and your organization. SPOILER ALERT: Some of you will think you're already prepared. This is me looking at you sharply over my eyeglass frames. How about we just pretend you aren't adequately prepared? Then maybe this preparation step will be helpful in inviting others you deem less prepared into the conversation. See what I did there? These other people may feel they're at least adequately prepared, but that doesn't mean they're perceived by others as competent. Preparation is a stage of this conversation that never ends, and frankly, it often never begins.

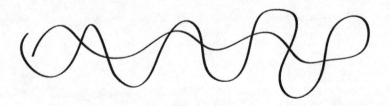

CHAPTER 5

Engage with Ideas

As Maria says in *The Sound of Music*, "Let's start at the very beginning, a very good place to start."

Any new idea has likely existed before, but we're inclined to just go with it without taking the opportunity to learn from its previous applications. More likely, we don't even think about it as a previously implemented practice, and our ego tells us that it's our new idea.

Either way, there's work to be done to best prepare, learn from, monitor, and adjust so that our "new" idea is set up for success. What better time to do this than before it's needed? It makes logical sense, but we often don't do the work.

I know, buzzkill Jess over here. But let's use a fun example to show you what I mean.

Figuratively join me in a child's elementary school classroom and think about a school culture that wants to implement Kindness Bingo. If you're a teacher, you may be familiar with some version of these two words being placed together or are familiar enough that your mind has created the idea of what this could mean. If the new principal brought up the idea, they may not know enough about the school's culture to make appropriate modifications that could set up the program to be more successful.

If I may, a suggestion here: If someone new to your organization is excitedly telling you about a "new" idea, do not interrupt; let the idea bubble up. However, do at some point suggest taking a thoughtful moment prior to the idea being implemented to see whether there's a way to both support the idea and prepare for possible outcomes for the specific stakeholders, in the case of Kindness Bingo, teachers, students, and families, that will be involved, as well as for how it will affect the school context. Hear the idea out, and let it filter through the cultural experience you have at the school knowing that others may experience something different than you might. Your new boss may be assuming that their last school and this school have similar cultures. You could learn something from the other setting while also determining what may need to be altered for here versus there.

To participate in Kindness Bingo, a student's parent or guardian fills in their initials on a Bingo card each day at home that the student does one act of kindness. What kind of preparation might make this initiative more successful? What kind of questions need to be asked so that the answers align with the culture of the classroom, school, home, or community? If your school has a lot of foster kids, legal guardians, or childcare givers, you may need to change the directions that go home with the activity. This is the kind of preparatory reflection process that's needed to understand the cultural experience at this school. Further conversation is needed about topics such as literacy skills, time available for the children and the adults in their lives, and how cooperative and supportive these adults are. You need to prepare by asking questions like these:

- Do these adults recognize, role model, and/or reward acts of kindness?
- What if there isn't a healthy relationship with an adult at home or even a stable home life consistent enough to get a daily signature?
- What if the child must teach their adult about kindness?

Once you get past these kinds of questions, the conversation can then move to asking more specific questions related to how incentivizing kindness could go wrong:

There's work to be done to best prepare, learn from, monitor, and adjust so that our "new" idea is set up for success. What better time to do this than before it's needed?

- What if students stop doing their "regular or normal" courteous habits, such as holding a door open or helping clean up a spill, for the rest of the day?
- By getting credit for only one act of kindness a day, might students be less inclined to do more acts of kindness as the day progresses?
- Should being kind even be gamified?
- Would a game of daily Blackout Bingo help increase the students' acts of kindness?
- What if the students were to sign each other's cards when they received an act of kindness?

Preparation won't answer all possible questions, yet it's a good practice. Because answers are likely to lead to more questions, preparation allows us to make more informed decisions while also remaining open to possibilities we hadn't thought about. We can know more and act better while also welcoming what we don't yet know. We can revise decisions, change direction, and update incentives, but only if we're prepared.

Before you implement Kindness Bingo, I recommend taking a moment to recognize what you know. Then leave an opening for what you know you don't know. This may be what keeps you awake at night, but I know many leaders who lose sleep over what they do actively know is happening in their organizations. My role is to open the rafters and make space for the never-ending amount of knowledge they don't even know they don't know.

Let's keep working with the analogy of Kindness Bingo being implemented in a school and see what kind of cultural understanding is needed to launch this program appropriately and successfully. We'll begin by asking these questions:

- How does organizational style influence the roll out of the program?
- What might change if a family suggested this idea? A teacher? A staff member? A student organization or group?

⑤ Elements of Culture

① Organizational Style

The way you are organized
not only communicates what
your company cares about
but determines what your
people are allowed to do.

② Artifacts

The physical elements your
organization produces
represent and reflect your
values.

③ Norms & Customs

Expectations, formal or
informal, about how to
behave. Every organization
has traditions, standard
operating procedures and
best practices that become
sedimented.

④ Language

Language structures our
thoughts including the
opportunities we perceive
and the threats we feel.

⑤ Belief & Values

Everyone in the organization
will share a common set of
beliefs, or they will find
themselves to be a bad "fit"
for the organization.

- Are we setting ourselves up for failure or being hypocritical? What about from the eyes of others instead of our own?

- What physical artifacts would make sense at this school, both with students and their home lives and with our staff?

- Are there any local or state rules associated with Kindness Bingo or similar programs?

- Has something like Kindness Bingo been done here before, and if so what can we learn from it?

- Are we clear in our instructions and expectations with all stakeholders?

- Do we role model or demonstrate kindness in our organization so that this is an oblivious extension of our school's beliefs and values?

If all these questions can come up about a take-home game, imagine what you're missing in your own organization. Let's prepare to work.

① Organizational Style

When I ask my clients about their organizational style, they often give me an organizational chart. Well, to be honest, I witness them struggle to find an organization chart. They usually delegate the task to someone else who eventually emails me a single graph that hasn't been updated since the 1980s. First, update your organizational chart. It's a visual representation of who reports, supports, and manages who on a team. Second, this isn't your organizational style. Organizational style is about how information is gathered, stored, shared, and hoarded and where influence shows up socially, usually outside of job titles or responsibilities. Don't know? You should. I'm not pushing for right answers here, or even a best practice, but an accurate portrayal of your organization's style:

- What is the functional structure or hierarchy of the organization?

Organizational style is about
how information is gathered,
stored, shared, and hoarded
and where influence shows
up socially, usually outside of
job titles or responsibilities.
Don't know? You should. I'm
not pushing for right answers
here, or even a best practice,
but an accurate portrayal
of your organization's style

- How does information, the distribution of resources, or even power move throughout the group?

- Is there a difference between functional power and social power? If so, how does this difference show up in daily practice in similar or varied manners?

- Is there a gender line connected to different kinds of power in your organization? What if you switch gender out for other characteristics such as age, tenure, language, education, or race?

- We talk about workplace ceilings, so while tracking the flow of power, are there stop gaps? Slippery fast-track slopes?

- Does the shape of the organization narrow or widen?

- Are there aspects closer to the centers of power while others are farther away?

If we use Kindness Bingo as an example, if the principal has an idea, who do they pass the idea along to? The teachers? Perhaps the teachers were there with the parents when the idea was presented, which would make for an open but very flat organization. If the principal were to instead pass the initiative along to a "second in command," such as an assistant principal, and then that person were to supervise the head teacher of each grade level, who in turn would pass the information along to other teachers, classroom aides, and parents, then there would be more of a hierarchical structure.

Both these strategies and many others can also coexist. The principal's idea may have come down from the superintendent or school board, or perhaps the parents' group leaders brought it forward. Regardless, understanding organizational style helps us track how power, resources, time, information, and energy flow throughout an organization, and this leaves space for the unknowns:

- How is this idea going to roll out?

- Who will lead the program?

- What does accountability for this program look like?

- Are key stakeholders on board?

Preparing for "What if X happens?" can differ when considered from the ground up or top down as well as organically or systematically. The difference is in an organizational style's impact on the cultural experience.

② Artifacts

How is the culture of your organization supported (or not) by the physical spaces, items, and tangibles used by your team members? The University of Tennessee has artifacts blanketing its physical location. Tennessee Orange and a serif-style capital T are absolutely everywhere on campus, down to the pattern in the carpet and the end tables in study lounges. Being so clear on colors, shapes, and styles must make decisions easier for their marketing team as well as their interior designers and architects. This doesn't mean that every decision is easier. It does, however, identify a common cultural experience, even to a stranger passing by in an airport.

Who uses which bathrooms in your organization? What about the parking spaces? The elevators and entrances? Printers and other equipment? Are there habits built around physical items in spaces that are unspoken until they're broken? When I worked at a hospital in one of the nurse's wards, for instance, there was one piece of equipment (a vein finder) that only the tenured nurses had the privilege of using. If this sounds weird, it's because even though hazing is wrong, it's a common practice across professions. The cliques of seasoned nurses would hide the equipment from the other nurses, and no floating or new nurse on the floor even knew it existed. While working with a patient, a newer nurse might be handed the gizmo and welcomed into that gaggle of nurses, like an initiation practice. When I challenged all this, I heard about how the newer nurses didn't think it was a big deal or preferred the older method anyway so they could stay out of the "nurse wars." And this was over a piece of equipment that could improve both the nurses' and the patients' experiences.

Never underestimate the power an item can enforce among the cultural lived experiences of a group, team, or organization.

③ Norms & Customs

Though how to manage workplace oddities is rarely written down, members of an organization quickly learn norms and customs from what they see. When such oddities go unchallenged, they become an organization's norms and customs.

Norms and customs are the live wires that keep group members bound and alert others when there's a violation. Perhaps there's a sign on the shared break room fridge that dictates how long someone can keep leftovers before they're tossed out. Maybe there's an approved schedule that rotates around the office, mandating who makes the morning coffee. Perhaps items without a name on them are free to whomever. These are unwritten rules in the workplace, just like how to handle morning coffee time at my house. Loren doesn't drink morning coffee out of any other mug but *his* coffee mug; he drinks tea or hot toddies out of any assortment of cups from our extensive selection, but morning coffee has unspoken rules.

Though norms and customs are a huge part of an organization's cultural experience, they often aren't identified until they're broken. For example, when I was living in Brooklyn, I wanted to have a stoop sale. I'd seen many stoop sales in my neighborhood, so I knew the pricing ranges pretty well and began gathering items to sell in my third-floor apartment. *Easy enough*, I thought. Yet that fateful Saturday was when I realized there was something I didn't know about stoop sales that someone else did. My most expensive item was a brocade quilted duvet cover that my cat had ripped a hole in, and therefore my feet would catch in it and rip it further. I brought it down first because I intended to lay it down as a decorative space holder for all my other items. After laying it out flat on the stoop steps and draping it up along the short fence, I returned inside for more items. When I came back it was gone. Stoop rules. It was on the sidewalk, unguarded, without a price tag. I was devastated because it was the most expensive item I was going to be selling. But I'd broken an unwritten rule.

This is a great example of not knowing something someone else knows that should be shared openly. Even when something is documented, we don't always remember it, and even documented rules are rarely kept up to date. When was the last time your organization reviewed its dress code? Sometimes this is an easier lift because fashions from decades ago (when the policy was last reviewed) are now back in fashion. Legal and safety requirements also change and evolve over time, though, so updates will likely need to be made to those areas to align with what occurs or ought to occur in the organization. Once you discuss these issues and update the rules to reflect the current norms and customs of your organization, then your organization can set up successful policies, procedures, protocols, emergency response systems, and new initiatives.

I often tell a story about a client's new CFO spending a full year preparing to be Charlie Chaplin for his company's office Halloween party. He'd been hired the previous year during the month of October, and somehow it had slipped by his onboarding process that the company took Halloween very seriously. He was the only one who showed up that year without a costume, so he spent the next year planning ahead. Imagine what he could've done with that time and energy instead of spending it trying to make up for a mistake he didn't even know he was making at the time.

To keep the conversation going through applying Kindness Bingo, we could look at the instructions of the game and how players win prizes. We could also check to see whether our school's parents, guardians, and students know how to play the game by asking questions like these.

- Are we assuming everyone understands how to play?
- What about the different ways of earning a Bingo, a blackout, and four corners? And what about the free space — do students get to be unkind once?

- Are the Bingo cards physical paper or electronic? If electronic, what if there isn't any access to the internet once a student leaves the school grounds?
- What if a student (or their parent or guardian) loses the Bingo card?
- What does "kindness" mean anyway, and who determines whether an act of supposed kindness qualifies for a Bingo spot?
- Can a single act of kindness qualify for more than one spot on a Bingo card?
- How do we account for those who aren't necessarily kinder but complete the act of marking the Bingo card more competitively or consistently?

So What if X happens? When all parties work with the same information at the same time about the same topic, they can prepare for a more informed and confident response process. All stakeholders need to get on the same Bingo card … I mean page.

4 Language

I remember doing my first corporate subcontractor interviews and repeatedly hearing the term "kaypeeyi." I wasn't sure how to spell "kaypeeyi," so eventually I asked someone (so brave!). They looked at me like I was dumb and explained that it's spelled "K-P-I," which stands for key performance indicators. "Oh, of course," I said, then quickly Googled what a key performance indicator is.

Coming out of education, I knew the term "learning objectives" and how school districts or state-specific standardized testing components are derived from data-driven instruction and shape the curriculum choices of actual teachers. So the subcontractors and I were speaking the same language; we just weren't using the same words.

In another case, I had a client show me where both bathrooms were in the warehouse in case I needed to go "number one or number two." Do we all know what "number one" and "number two" mean? Who knew this would be so relevant when picking which bathroom to use at a warehouse? Because this language is assumed, does that mean I'm supposed to remember? And how do I confirm that I remember correctly? Perhaps there are artifacts such as air freshener in the restroom to guide my language use?

When you're in Tennessee, the Volunteer State, it's common to hear "Go Vols!" The expression can be triggered by the sight of a particular color of orange or the shape of a particular T. Those familiar with the sights and the language know that when they hear the expression, it means that someone is acknowledging the Volunteers or the "Vols," a term used to refer to sports teams at the University of Tennessee. Similarly, as a University of South Carolina alum, I know there's an appropriate time and place for me to say, "Go Cocks!" Taken out of context, though, that would be very strange to hear. Language matters, and it plays a significant role in understanding and affirming organizational culture.

> When all parties work with the same information at the same time about the same topic, they can prepare for a more informed and confident response process. All stakeholders need to get on the same Bingo card ... I mean page.

"Beano!" is what a player used to call out when they believed they won at the game we now commonly refer to as Bingo. Originating from an Italian lottery, the game was originally called Beano in the US. But when a toy salesman named Edwin. S. Lowe heard a player accidentally shout "Bingo!" instead of "Beano!," he officially changed the name of the game.

Today, yelling "Beano!" means the same thing as yelling "Bingo!," but only if you know how to play the game. And even if you do, perhaps you've never seen written Bingo rules but learned how to play from watching someone else or having others teach you. I myself learned different ways of winning at Bingo from a Drag Bingo event. When I entered the event, I was very comfortable with the game and decided to play multiple cards at once. Then I started hearing new language being used and was introduced to entirely new ways of winning the game. I had to ask for help, though I thought I knew what I was doing. We learn how to do things in all sorts of ways, and each way is dependent on the words we use.

Language also evolves and changes over time, so various initiatives may need refreshing to accurately describe the work being done while also attracting the correct participants. Think about the phone protocol trainings you may have experienced. I was provided a literal script of what to say when I answered my office phone, put someone on hold, transferred a call, or accepted a transferred call. This is no longer commonplace knowledge because landlines are almost obsolete.

Likewise, a prescribed notion of "professionalism" and its application in your workplace may no longer be a common assumption, especially if there are remote workers. Standing meetings came about to make quick and efficient use of shift changes, like a huddle during a sporting event, but what do we do when our direct reports can't stand for 15 minutes in the same hallway? Is the point of a quick touch-base session without the comfort of a chair, or is it to make it a regular habit to touch base about the meaning of the word "standing?"

Going back to Kindness Bingo, I'd assume that the biggest discussion would be about what types of activities would earn a signature and how this would be validated by others. What if someone doesn't understand the words you think they ought to know? What if X happens and the party with the information is 100 percent confident that the other party understands what to do even though they don't? Your organizational culture dictates whether communication is clear, information is understood correctly, and responding actions are in line with expectations. Whether you know it or not, feeling permitted to ask questions and making assumptions that someone else in fact does or doesn't need more information is how your organization's culture is currently working.

Your organizational culture dictates whether communication is clear, information is understood correctly, and responding actions are in line with expectations.

⑤ Beliefs & Values

Workplace culture shifted in many ways when organizations began to broaden their profit- or shareholder-driven focus to include stakeholders across an entire value chain of the life span of a given product (move over Milton Friedman and make room for E. Edward Freeman). Please do not read this shift as an improvement for all employees, surrounding community members, and those involved in the creation of said product, but it's been a fundamental shift, nonetheless.

Profit suddenly found itself at the center of a trifecta of competing, yet supposedly complimentary areas of focus: profit, people, and planet (often referred to in business management classes as the three Ps). The three Ps show up in any organization's beliefs and values, as demonstrated by highly polished and overly market-driven annual reports. What you need to be asking yourself is this:

- In addition to shareholders making a return on their investment, what else did the organization do for the world?
- How did the organization make choices to reinvest profits back into the surrounding communities?
- What social ail does the organization focus on solving?

These are not little questions. As a new form of competition, corporate social responsibility programs are differentiating organizations from one another. This is another way that human rights are applied to an organization, responsibility comes with liability, and freedom of speech expands to include political donations.

Perhaps more importantly, corporate social responsibility programs often anthropomorphize an organization's beliefs and values into competitive differentiations in terms of what it means to be a shareholder, consumer, or employee, or even to have a physical building in a particular area. Getting picked for a Google facility is great for an community's reputation, real estate values, and property values, for example, and being an Apple product user instead of an Android user means something culturally that connects our user humanness to an organization's personified characteristics. Similarly, being a Subaru driver carries social weight that differs from that of early adopters of the PT Cruiser (shout-out to my ZZ Top fans out there). In other words, organizations and products have human characteristics and even more human rights than some humans.

The beliefs and values of an organization permeate its workplace culture and personify a story out into the world. Though both iPhones and Androids use the same natural resources mined from our planet, are built using the same bits and pieces shipped from all around the world, and are packaged and sent to end users in the same way, the social stories of the two are different. The differences are communicated through intentional marketing campaigns that increase sales and develop brand loyalty that supersedes matters such as quality and return on investment.

So, if your organization's beliefs and values are what binds the three Ps as aspects of your organization's overall function, why are they still ambiguous? I encourage my clients to put a stake in the ground and do the following:

◎ State their beliefs and values, but
   ↠ mean them and
   ↠ act on them.

◎ Use these beliefs and values to align the organization's
   ↠ recruitment,
   ↠ hiring,
   ↠ promotion,
   ↠ probation, and
   ↠ termination of its people.

◎ Decide what to do
   ↠ to improve conditions on the planet, and
   ↠ to turn a profit through the value chain of their work
   ↠ to align with workers' rights
   ↠ to improve conditions on the plant, and
   ↠ to turn a profit.

Simple.

Over the past few years, the idea of purpose has been added to the three Ps, and they're now often referred to as the four Ps. And yet, here we are. We often don't know what we value or believe until it's tested. It seems logical, then, that we could do our own testing before a high-stakes situation arises and the media suss out any misalignment. But who am I? Oh, just an outsider who's hit the same wall hundreds of times with clients who aren't interested in doing the preparatory work before it's needed and then get caught off guard in an emergency when they have the most to lose. Rather than doing the important preparation work, they lost resources, time, people, and profits that have taken years to build.

Preparation is the best investment any organization can make regarding the many X options in their biggest fear, "What if X happens?" Metaphorically, Kindness Bingo sounds like a great marketing campaign that consumers, employees, and stakeholders alike can wrap their hearts and minds around, so it launches as a campaign serving two conflicting purposes:

1. "Hey, stakeholders, look at us! We value kindness."

2. "Teaching kindness is needed, wanted, and expected here."

This initiative could then cast a shadow on industry competitors who may not value kindness. Those that don't instill Kindness Bingo could look less kind or launch a counter campaign that they "don't have to teach or gamify kindness because only kindness is permitted here in the first place." Suddenly kindness isn't at the center of either campaign, but one-upmanship and competition have taken center stage. The actual user experience has yet to garner the attention needed to see whether any of this makes any sense to begin with.

Occasionally I work with clients who want to do some of this preparation or culture work because a particular competitor or benchmark organization shared an internal problem, and the client wants to get ahead of the concern. These benchmark mishaps motivate leadership to initiate these "What if X happens?" conversations, but they usually peter out pretty quickly. It's challenging to have conversations about the unknown, the assumed commonalities, and the like across power dynamics. At best, who leads these preparatory, hypothetical, scenario-based

Grab a pen and a sheet of paper.

Or even better, download this worksheet — and other handy tools from this book — at goodenoughnow.com/freebies

Six Elements of Culture Change Framework

Culture is how people know what to do even when there isn't anyone around telling them how to behave. It is our invisible guide, and it is ALWAYS reflective of an underlying value system.

VARIABLE	IDEAS	YOU
ORGANIZATIONAL STYLE: The way you are organized not only communicates what your company cares about but determines what your people are allowed to do.	Implement systems that incentivize and hold units accountable for working together and communicating.	
ARTIFACTS: The physical elements your organization produces represents your values.	Develop and implement plans for full staffing and resourcing of support offices.	
CUSTOMS: Every organization has traditions, standard operating procedures and best practices that become sedimented.	Develop a sound, multi-modal DEI curriculum that leverages existing resources and outside sources.	
NORMS: Expectations, formal or informal, about how to behave.	Leadership is essential. Publicly support both individuals and units doing this work.	
LANGUAGE: Language structures out thoughts including the opportunities we perceive and the threats we feel.	Systemically listen to stakeholders to help create assessable action items that support inclusion.	
BELIEF & VALUES: Everyone in the organization will share a common set of beliefs, or they will find themselves to be a bad "fit" for the organization.	State your beliefs often. Change message from "We care" to "We'll fight for you."	

conversations is a decision usually delegated to a subcommittee made up of representatives from all areas of an organization. Typically, however, a few thinkers are given a quick timeline to run through scenarios to at least cover liability or look on top of the issue. The surface-level findings are summarized into a five-minute presentation that rarely results in implementation.

If a program is built out of these hypothetical discussions, they don't reflect the needs of the whole organization, they're underfunded, and they're filed as "other duties assigned" rather than considered a service to the organization. They're often toothless by lacking any authority, and they're the first initiatives to be deprioritized or "sunsetted" when something seemingly more important comes to the forefront.

Identifying your own beliefs and values and how they serve as stakes in the ground when you make decisions and inform your choices and responses (or don't) is work that only you can do. And it costs nothing.

check-in

If you haven't done this yet, I highly recommend you grab a piece of paper and map out who are your organization's stakeholders. Think about all parties that are involved or impacted for each location and then across your industry. This process will also illuminate who is impacted by your existence from start to finish. Identifying your stakeholders will also map out your organization's value chain. If you build a widget think step by step from the ground, to shipping, to assembly, distribution, purchase, use, storage, recycle, reuse, disposal, of that widget across the item's lifetime. This will also help identify more stakeholders. Now you know your audience — who you should consider because they are watching you and waiting for you to take the lead.

CHAPTER 6

Use Apologies as Assessments

The most telling evidence of an organization's self-awareness is its own apology statements. I do quite a bit of work crafting apologies for organizations that have found themselves on the wrong side of shifting social and workplace norms. I'm always pleased to be part of the exercise because it indicates a potential for growth.

Why do I find myself helping people apologize so often? Because we're in a time of rapid societal change — for the better — and making mistakes is an absolutely inevitable part of functioning in society. Atoning for them properly is the tricky bit.

Is this how it comes out when you're apologizing?:

> "I'm sorry *if* you were offended." vs. "I'm sorry *that* you were offended."

If so, you're missing the mark. If statements not only take on zero responsibility but say nothing about the organization's beliefs and values. In turn, this says a lot about the workplace's culture and how the organization wasn't prepared for the situation that warranted the apology in the first place.

A well-crafted apology includes some key ingredients. Humility is the obvious one, but knowing *how* to apologize and being clear on the outcome are also nonnegotiable.

Remove "If" from Your Apology

Take a moment to assess your most recent apology statement, press release, or all-team memo. Go fetch it. I'll wait. If you haven't ever apologized or can't remember the last time, well, that says a lot too! Perhaps you have a statement about an important stakeholder's, leader's, or board member's passing or their exit from the company. Surely you have a statement about school shootings, acts of violence, disasters, catastrophic accidents, or failures on your organization's part. Anything will do.

Now, using your writing program's search or find feature, run a search on your apology for the word "if." If there's an "if" in your apology, you're already doomed! You cannot successfully articulate your beliefs and values with any degree of credibility if you are wavering on your responsibility. An apology needs to be a declarative statement, and it needs to align with the cultural experience in your organization.

If you've said or done something that offended someone else, you don't get to act like you didn't. Doing so only invalidates the pain the other person experienced and indicates your denial that something actually happened. Even if you didn't experience it firsthand, it did happen. Otherwise you wouldn't be searching for a way to apologize, would you?

If you're hedging your apology with an "if," it's a clear demonstration that you

- Are not taking responsibility for your actions;
- Have not put yourself in the other person's shoes and thought about how you would feel at the receiving end of your words or actions;

If there's an "if" in
your apology, you're
already doomed!

- Have not really taken time to understand the nature of the offense; and

- Are not prepared to take responsibility using your own beliefs and values as guides for your organization's culture.

Do not misunderstand me. You do not have to feel the same way they do; in fact, you almost certainly cannot. You just have to stretch your empathy and understanding muscles to reach into the emotional and intellectual space the other person inhabits.

There are some simple steps you can take when crafting apologies that will not only assuage the pain of the person you've hurt but open the door for greater understanding. And with any luck, you'll avoid making the same mistake.

Four Safe Assumptions to Guide Your Apologies

When you're crafting apologies, it's wise to operate under these four assumptions:

1. An apology cannot be "if needed." It either is or it is not.
2. We have all done things out of ignorance and may not even remember.
3. We are responsible for our collective past, present, and future regardless of whether we did an egregious act.
4. We are not entitled to anything, despite our interest in learning.

Let's take a closer look at assumptions three and four, because they're extremely important.

If you're on board with assumption three, then you hold responsibility for the constructs and rules we all navigate in society.

Stay with me here …

I do a great deal of volunteer work with fraternity and sorority members across the country, both on campus and in their national offices and councils. During a visit a few years ago, I worked with a fraternity that had nearly lost a new member to alcohol poisoning. When one student asserted to me, "It's not my fault the kid didn't know his limits," I explained to him that I feel responsible for the health and safety of all living things on the planet. I wasn't the person who tapped the keg at his party, but I acknowledge that I am part of a society that enables someone to feel the pressure to make poor choices. That includes allowing someone to nearly drink themselves to death. For that, I bear responsibility. I benefit from the systems that allow us to make these poor choices, and I must commit to doing better as a human being. The student and I spoke further, ultimately recommitting to the higher standards for life when we affiliated with our fraternal organizations.

Regarding assumption four, nothing takes away from the impact of an apology like a quid pro quo: "I've said I'm sorry, now what do I get in return?" An apology is transaction neutral; it doesn't add credit to your account. If you've explored the reason your words or actions were offensive, sought to do better in the future, and apologized sincerely, you're well on your way to healing yourself and opening the door for the other person to heal as well. Just do not demand evidence that the other person feels requited. That's not how it works. You can be a role model by fulfilling your promises. When you don't, apologize genuinely.

Politicians can be the worst culprits of blameless and conditional apologies, but we do it in business and our personal lives too. We see it most obviously in politics because the participants are public figures and thus their lives and choices are on display. And we feel they owe us their good behavior by virtue of our vote and their paycheck. But they feel that we owe them our loyalty once they've apologized for their blunders, whether it's a tone-deaf comment regarding gender or race, outright fraud, or illegal activities. You are not owed anything by the person you've wronged just because you've apologized.

If you've done your organization's preparatory culture work, then taking responsibility is easy. You know what you stand for and can accept when you misstep, fail, or hurt someone. You also have clarity about when and why you're trying to accomplish something and can double down on this focus, even challenging others to hold you accountable.

When you're clear on your own cultural experience, you can role model for others in your industry how to do the same.

Offering an apology statement may be one of the most common performative responses that my clients attempt too quickly. Consequently, they end up doing more harm than good. Wanting to make something better or alleviate harm and wanting to apologize are often closely tied to needing forgiveness. For many, being forgiven is the ultimate absolution of responsibility, but their apology statements often reek of displacing responsibility just to make the situation go away or to save face. Instead, they need to recognize that they don't know their organizational culture nor how their own experience aligns (or doesn't) with that of their coworkers or between departments, across locations, among users, and at multiple consumer touch points. This isn't bad news but just news to them.

Understanding that you don't know the organizational culture of your own organization is a fantastic starting place. Being curious about what it's like for others outside of your own experience is an important skill in leadership. Staying open to previously unknown information bridges power dynamics and social differences, and it allows a leader to lead everyone instead of just themselves as well as hope (or assume) that others are following suit. To guide your preparation for the unknowns that have yet to come into focus, I encourage you to nurture this sense of curiosity in others.

Get to work. Your work is in broadening your organizational culture, which spans the actual structure as well as the style and shape of your organization; determining whether there are consistencies and incongruencies among the artifacts, customs and norms, and language within your organization; and aligning all of that with the organization's beliefs and values.

Don't let someone else tell your story, especially during an emergency when it's too late. Keep asking questions so that you're so prepared to answer the "What if X happens?" question that you can roll through a few options yourself, listen to others' ideas, and still look for more possibilities that not only align with but showcase the actual cultural experience of being a valued part of your organization.

Lunch Yoga

An often well-intentioned, yet triggering event while at work is providing a lunch yoga program for employees. What better way to provide office staff with a way to focus on their mental and physical health than to have a local yoga instructor come to the office during lunch? The motive is clear, and the health of employees is even incentivized by offers of lower insurance rates for healthier employees.

However, not everyone is physically able to do yoga, and some prefer to engage in such physical activities in private, not with friends or family, let alone with the folks they work with. When the program began rolling out at several of my clients' offices, there was an uptick in sexual harassment, fraternization at work, and unwanted comments about employees' bodies. And employees who took the time to do yoga needed additional time away from their work responsibilities to change into workout clothes, do the program, shower, put on work attire, and eat lunch. All of this began to affect employee morale.

Additionally, employees who wanted to "get ahead" dismissed lunch yoga as a slacker activity and began working through lunch, which led to unhealthy habits. The choice of instructor also needs more attention to ensure instruction and employee customization doesn't lead to injury.

If leadership were to visibly participate in the lunch yoga workouts, encourage their staff to take additional time for lunch, and role model what a healthy work-life balance looks like, it's possible that the program could motivate and incentivize teams to work together, support one another, and encourage breathing room, breaks, and the like. But upper-level managers and supervisors rarely participate because they don't want to be in sports clothing or navigate changing with employees.

Namaste right here in my office, thank you.

While working through what it takes to understand your own workplace culture deeply, you will see that lots of knowns and unknowns are going to bubble up. For some, these bubbles inspire new ideas and innovative tactics, while others may take a minute to identify complex feelings, triggers, post-traumatic responses, and the like. Both can be distracting and helpful at the same time.

Deciding what's mandated as paid time away from work responsibilities while at work can be ambiguous. Now second-guessing enters a new initiative, and that leads to anxiety. "Damned if you do and damned if you don't," is at the root of most organization's fears.

You may be asking, "Do we really have to solve all of this?" I know, it can be a lot. But the answer is already in front of you. Whatever you're doing or not doing, whatever you're ignoring or focusing on, is already something you may or may not recognize is having a direct impact on your organization's culture. The gaps, misalignments, and frankly the hypocrisy are not lost on those out there who are navigating these troubled waters. Jump on in, the water is too dark to see the bottom, and so far nothing too bad has happened. At least not recently.

Let's say instead that leadership is anxious about a forecasted recession coming in the next few years and fears significant layoffs. They could look around at other industry partners to see what they're doing to prepare for their organization's future. Opening lines of communication to share what they're doing and learn from others is an awesome and free way to shorten a learning curve. It's also a great way to decrease the chances of the competition looking greener, thus risking talent loss.

By harnessing our ideas and feelings, we can recognize, share, and support our fears and anxiety across an organization and an entire industry, alleviating scarcity and developing a sense of shared identity. Remember, we are shooting for a complex pattern of disruption, where everything happens at once, with lots of points of entry – just begin somewhere and pedal in the same direction with your stakeholders.

Part 2

Recognize

Part 2: Recognize

prepare

recognize

respond

What if it happens?

Hey! There is a landmine here!

typical response   Hold on, let me get my shoe-shining kit.

better response

Well that's terrifying!
Are you ok? We don't stand for this.

When we're caught off guard, we feel all kinds of pressure, both within ourselves (internal) and concerning others (external). We often end up battling with ourselves that we should've known something or been more prepared somehow but weren't. Externally, others may assume we're more experienced or have an understanding that we don't, and to meet expectations we may feel forced to act accordingly. Internally, we might either gulp or cheer, freeze or decide to act.

For now, let's just focus on recognizing what happens when we develop our skill of noticing something that hasn't been noticed before, or knowing something we didn't know we didn't know. After all, who's more responsible for our own motivations, worries, or ambitious goals than us? Others may have an agenda we feel we're obligated to complete, and we can put that same pressure onto others. It's incumbent upon each of us to understand our own sense of responsibility and what we do with our own agency. But only by first doing our own recognition work related to the pain and suffering we may not be experiencing firsthand can we lead others to do good too.

CHAPTER 7

Face the Unknown

What if the problems being reported in your organization are actually happening? What if you're the last to know? What if you did know but didn't do anything about it, and here you are again? This is your chance to disrupt your own comfort level and recognize the resources you and your organization have at your fingertips to lead the way in doing better and role model for others to do the same.

After my keynotes and workshops, I almost always get the same question: "What about *them*?" I respond with, "What if *you* are someone's 'them'?"

Waiting for "them" to do something different is how we got here. If you are someone's them, it would follow that "they" are waiting on *you* to do something different. Most of us barely have control of ourselves, so I'm not sure why we think we have any control over someone else, especially someone we have such disdain for that we point our finger and snarl as we say the word "them." We must do whatever is necessary to recognize that we are also part of the dynamic being questioned. To help you do this, I'll walk through some tough questions, both for you and your organization. Then we can define the individuals and the competitors in your industry that you're waiting on to be different. Ultimately, you are as responsible as they are, and you have control of your influence to elevate expectations across your industry and beyond.

To begin taking responsibility and having influence, let's start by turning our focus to who and how you are when you show up inside your organization as well as how your leadership team shows up with stakeholders.

We question our own role in DEI initiatives because we haven't done enough reflecting on our own cultural experiences, so we find ourselves feeling pressure to react to something we don't even understand. We are sensitive and highly reactive as global entities as much as we are as individuals, and we can use this new recognition to build bridges of empathy or actively reach out to others to offer and accept support through collaboration.

Sounds great Jess, but what about *them*?

I hear you! Those you identify as "them" could be an excellent source of support, guidance, and clarity in accomplishing your own expectations. Furthermore, they could see you in a similar light. Recognizing this potential elevates these relationships from industry competitors and benchmarks to invaluable partnerships that can leave lasting legacies on humanity. We need to recognize this potential in "them" so that we can aim to make better connections instead of measuring success competitively. Moreover, we need to understand our own limitations and intentions and observe the successes of others.

Actively seeking guidance from outsiders isn't a typical industry best practice, yet most major innovative advances take an existing product made by someone else and apply it in different ways. We can utilize others for our benefit and can easily and intentionally share responsibility with others to produce unexpected, if not unimaginable, outcomes. We don't have to know exactly how to do this, we just need to recognize that it's not only possible; it is essential. Collaboratively supporting one another leads to significantly better results that aren't rooted in winning or being right. Together we can ask questions, challenge best practices, and develop even better ways that align with our intended workplace culture. We can transform into who we've been claiming to be all along.

Every client I have ever worked with has documented norms and functional customs that vary from office to office, department to department, and location to location. No amount of preparation will ever align everyone and every element to an identical experience. That isn't a goal worth striving for anyway because it's a time-suck, resource-waster, and the answer to the problem has been picked over too many times. The human variable itself depends on variation, nimbleness, flexibility, preference, and resourcefulness to be creative, innovative, and good at solving problems.

If things aren't going to be uniform, then noticing the differences should be easy, right? But how does someone recognize a problem they don't experience themselves? Great question! We can go back to the main question, What if X happens? You don't have to experience X yourself to work through what could or should happen if X occurs.

A great example of this is when, in my first job after graduate school in Oregon, my supervisor would constantly ask worst-case-scenario questions as tests to see what we'd do. There wasn't really a risk because we couldn't answer these hypotheticals incorrectly. I think I was particularly good at these, and though there was a lot about her supervisory style I learned not to be like, I really did value her ability to ask thought-provoking questions. As she was a supervisor, I imagined this process also gave her a window into her staff's strengths, weaknesses, creativity, and resourcefulness as well as their fears and biases. Well, one morning during our staff retreat at a remote camp site, she asked me a fairly catastrophic question. I remember my student staff was cleaning up from breakfast and I was taking out the garbage when the supervisor asked me to sit by the camp's fire pit. She gave me the known facts and asked me what I would do. The conversation played out something like this:

"Jess, I got one for you. What do you think we should do as a staff if several commercial airliners have been hijacked, others are still missing, and we may be under attack as a country?" I took a drag from my cigarette, thought for a beat or two, and said this:

We are currently at a remote campsite without good cell service or television. We have about two hundred student leaders in addition to six other staff members, and there are four people working the campsite. If we leave early and head back to campus, everyone can do what they need to do to check on their families since people are from all over the place. There are three student staff members flying internationally who are scheduled to arrive at our major airport tomorrow, and they'll need to be checked on as well. So, I would say, let's pack up, head back, give everyone several hours of time, then reconvene in the common room for a status update as a full staff. This plan could roll out within the next ten or fifteen minutes, with each of us telling our own staff of the changes and limited knowledge we have of what has happened, seemingly on the East Coast thus far.

I calmly put my cigarette out and looked at her, thinking that these scenarios are getting really intense.

She clapped her hands together and said, "Okay. I'll pull the other directors together now. Stay here."

As she walked away, I realized this was real. I had to replay the details she'd shared and whatever off-the-cuff response I'd just made up. I'd given an answer to a question I didn't know was real. I had way more questions, and just had to trust the process.

It was at this time, now referred to as 9/11, that I realized preparation is helpful even if it means pulling from other areas of our lives. And it's not in place of recognizing when we've arrived at a new experience. I'd never experienced war, and my student staff had known me for less than four days, yet I was their leader. I'd been on this job for only a little over a month, but here I was pulling together all the lived experiences I'd had and waiting to see what happened next.

Buckle up buttercup!

If you think asking or answering hypothetical questions is rough, I challenge you with recognizing something you haven't experienced and likely never will.

Most of the clients I work with are very well-resourced and have the authority (and sometimes the respect) to do just about anything they want inside an organization. Ultimately, these are the folks who fund DEI initiatives, set standards, and work to align an organization's strategic goals, forecasting, and stakeholder demands with lived experiences. Yet statistically, these same decision makers are the most removed from the daily pain, suffering, marginalization, oppression, harassment, and inadequacy of resources that the initiatives are often targeting. Theme months, employee resource groups (ERGs), internal Slack channels, and the like are created to acknowledge or highlight diversity within an organization. But none of this comes without more questions:

- How is funding determined?
- Is funding the same across the board regardless of the number of participants?
- How are we defining "participation"?

Funding could also be allocated based on the number of X that self-identify as X:

- What if one person identifies with more than one group?
- What if someone identifies as something that doesn't have a group?
- How is labor rewarded for building out, supporting, and organizing programming, or are these actions considered voluntary?

Chances are, the decision makers are making these choices on paper or outsourcing them to other subordinates who'll then also make choices, either on paper to be objective or person-to-person to be subjective. Either way, the deciders often don't experience the problem these solutions are addressing. Even if one group has a similar identity to or a shared lived experience with that of another group, the power dynamics are different. You know this. If you don't, this is a good place to start recognizing that you can't ever be "one of them" without actually being one of "them." That's why you get paid the big bucks.

Let's take a breath.

Recognizing that you didn't or don't recognize something is a lot, and no amount of preparation readies you to feel unready. In every email, every phone call, and every stakeholder interaction we have, there's a good chance we don't know what's going to happen. We like to feel prepared, at least until we're told to prepare for something that hasn't happened. Being caught off guard isn't always fun. I am "Team Curiosity" and lean into the unknown, yet I still remember — more than 20 years later — putting out that cigarette while trying to remember what had transpired because I didn't realize the hijacked airplanes were real.

Many feelings will come up as we adjust to a new way of looking at DEI. Our job here is to recognize them and then harness the unknown until we can recognize it as something we didn't previously know, but now do.

Recognizing what we don't know is tricky. This investigative curiosity is similar to being open to determining what you know you don't know and what you will never know you don't know. This isn't an exercise in futility, however. Recognition is an imperative skill that requires practice. Here's a starting place for you and your team. SPOILER ALERT: if you don't have immediate and similar answers, there's work to be done:

> **Recognizing that you didn't or don't recognize something is a lot, and no amount of preparation readies you to feel unready.**

- What can you do now to lessen ambiguity for those who may be experiencing anxiety or are fearful of what could happen?

- Even if you're worried about being in the wrong place, feel unsafe or lost, or have a sense of scarcity, how can you help others feel welcome?

- How can you provide a space for important conversations where everyone belongs?

- What are you doing to acknowledge that no one is good at DEI, yet it's the right thing to do?

- Immediate results will be expected, so can you recognize in advance the fears your leadership team, employees, consumers, vendors, and other stakeholders in the surrounding community could experience?
- What are you planning to do to take your own and their fears into account?

Let me ask again...

If you tapped into your social hubs, community influencers, and strong personalities within the organization, would they align with your leadership's answers?

If not, know that others are turning to you for guidance and leadership. You are not expected to know everything, but you are expected to be honest and transparent, both with your stakeholders and across your industry.

You are not expected to know everything, but you are expected to be honest and transparent, both with your stakeholders and across your industry.

CHAPTER 8

Recognize "Me"

You may be familiar with the term "trigger" to identify a moment when someone else's reaction (or yours, for those playing at the advanced level) is rooted in something deeper and comes off as disproportionate to the situation at hand. In customer service trainings, an example is often used of someone at an information booth who grows frustrated after being asked the same question too many times. Similarly, I know enough about myself to know that when I'm walking through a busy airport, I get triggered and grow increasingly more frustrated as I have to start and stop walking quickly while navigating other travelers. Instead of blowing up and taking it out on the seventh person who casually stops in the middle of the walkway, I have to control the pileup of my own frustrations. Typically, I chant to myself, "Walk with purpose." If needed, I can say this out loud and be less awful to people just because I'm in a hurry.

We can bite a person's head off as we answer the same question or they repeat an annoying behavior for the zillionth time, or we can choose to remain calm and remember that we're there to provide information and support. We may not always be in control of our feelings and emotional reactions, but we are in control of our responses. I don't know whether this is possible all the time, but it's our responsibility to notice when we do and when we don't have it under control and when it's easier or harder — hopefully before we blow up.

Hope isn't a business plan. Before we can do anything else, we need to address both our personal and our organization's sources of fear that are preventing the recognition of a problem we may or may not be experiencing. Ideally, we can build up these skills without getting defensive or dismissive of a previously unknown problem that a stakeholder is experiencing within our scope of responsibility.

Each of us is responsible for understanding our own vulnerabilities that often surface due to ambiguity, scarcity, fear of missing out, second-guessing, and anxiety. If we do the work necessary to recognize how these elements show up in our behaviors, it's easier to identify how our vulnerabilities appear in our organization.

Ambiguity

March of 2020 will forever serve as an example of how society deals with ambiguity. When the COVID-19 pandemic hit, most organizations didn't have access to a stakeholder who'd survived the Spanish Flu and could provide ideas regarding how to cope with a pandemic, so collectively we were left to punt. Details unfolded while we reacted. No one waited to figure out best practices or did a survey with follow-up focus groups. We acted as best as we could, and we were responding to changing mandates and political and economic pressures. We recognized the need to act, and the ambiguity was less scary because everyone was experiencing it all at the same time. The factions that resulted picked their responses and often doubled down on working from evolving and often contradictory information.

You likely remember the ambiguous fear we each felt individually, and honestly, we as a whole are still processing it. Reflecting organizationally may provide enough distance for some objectivity. Here at home, for instance, I quickly learned how to keynote and emcee virtually, which meant using dongles and web cameras and speaking to blacked-out screens. I entered into what can only be described as severe scope creep

March of 2020 will forever serve as an example of how society deals with ambiguity. When the COVID-19 pandemic hit, most organizations didn't have access to a stakeholder who'd survived the Spanish Flu and could provide ideas regarding how to cope with a pandemic, so collectively we were left to punt. Details unfolded while we reacted. No one waited to figure out best practices or did a survey with follow-up focus groups. We acted as best as we could.

to support my clients by helping hundreds, if not thousands, of their event participants get through a shared sense of ambiguity, all while serving as a resource of clarity. During this time, Loren and I developed a COVID-19 motto: "Clarity is kindness." No one knew exactly what this meant, but we knew what it didn't mean. This was enough to work with when free-falling into the unknown. Being crystal clear about what was known, expected, and possible was just enough kindness to share some light during dark times.

Knowing we don't know something is unsettling at best. Recognizing that no one knows something or, worse yet, that someone knows but you don't, can be triggering and lead to reactions that may not make a lot of sense (such as hoarding toilet paper). Spinning our fears into the finest thread of clarity can settle a sense of ambiguity so that we can recognize what's happening around us. Only then can we react proportionally through our own lived experiences while also learning from others.

I often think about my clients who took successful action during the pandemic, such as micro distilleries who instantly reconfigured from manufacturing vodka to pumping out hand sanitizer.

I often think about my clients who took successful action during the pandemic, such as micro distilleries who instantly reconfigured from manufacturing vodka to pumping out hand sanitizer and restaurants that carved out outdoor seating areas in their parking lots, created pickup windows from doorways, and offered catering to first responders. We didn't know much, which was certainly scary, yet we were able to work with what we did know at the time by recognizing what was needed and what we could do about the needs of others.

In terms of DEI initiatives, we don't have a proven road map that gives up a step-by-step approach to success; the path is ambiguous at best. Yet, doing the right thing is always the right thing to do.

Scarcity

There's a parable that describes two types of people at a pizza buffet when it's obvious there isn't enough pizza for the number of people who'll be eating. Some pass, and some take half a piece or one slice at most. Seeing the disparity, others take their seconds on the first go-through so that they aren't left without.

Scarcity is real for many and imagined for others. Yet those who've experienced real scarcity may never update their feelings as their situation evolves and changes, so their mindsets may not align with current realities. Perceived scarcity can trigger reactions that may or may not seem rational, yet here we are. It's our responsibility to navigate how scarcity impacts our individual and organizational reactions.

A technology company I worked with prior to the pandemic wanted only the best of the best programmers in the world. They believed there was a scarcity of talent and spent a fortune on perks for their employees. Chefs cooked four meals a day, and pet and childcare were provided at every location, as was a dry-cleaning service, full gym access, and much, much more. When I asked the young employees what parts of their lives weren't owned by the company, they made fun of my Gen X-ness. Perhaps that showed my own sense of scarcity connected to my own agency and autonomy as I wouldn't want to trade in my privacy and independence to a company no matter how fresh the sashimi was. Following the pandemic, at this same company, 100 percent of the employees I interviewed began working remotely and had zero intention of returning to the company's prime real estate.

Scarcity informs our responses, and it's fueled by our own history swirling around as fear. Growing up in the South, I'm used to having to run out for milk, bread, and toilet paper at the first rumor of a storm coming. And I never experienced food insecurity growing up, not while serving in the Peace Corps, through graduate school, nor in my now grown-up life. Loren had a very different experience. Because he didn't grow up with a lot of excess food, he often made fun of me buying food in bulk, even if it saved money. As a scholarship swimmer, he closely monitored his weight, and he forced himself to eat more than usual to make the goal each Monday morning. In addition, his Peace Corps service was in an area of Nepal with significant food insecurity. As we sheltered in place during COVID-19, his first concern was a lack of food for us and the dogs. Finally, my bulk-purchasing habit came in handy! Even though we never had to skip a meal, his past experiences with scarcity brought up real insecurities and fear in him that I needed to recognize and support.

There's a misconception that power dynamics shifting across DEI initiatives leads to power scarcity, and this is not the case. Again, restructuring power by giving voice to those who've been silenced is always the right thing to do.

Fear of Missing Out

The fear of missing out, or FOMO, fuels a lot of reactions from people and organizations. Individually, we want to experience or possess everything at once, but we have to make a choice. We don't want to be responsible for the decision we make nor lose track of a missed opportunity that might come around again or might be better missed altogether. Not knowing what the best decision is can be upsetting, to say the least, but sometimes we simply cannot know. When given a choice, we can know only some of the options we have to choose from. When there are options we can't even fathom, fear mounts. Regardless, we must gather the information necessary for us to make a choice we can stick with. This is much easier said than done.

When I worked at New York University, one of the two largest real estate owners in Manhattan, it came to the upper administration's attention that a student was blogging about being homeless. I attended a meeting about this during which the conversation began to drift into a FOMO. In a conversation addressing one student's housing (or lack thereof) situation, administrators who likely had never experienced

Perceived scarcity can trigger reactions that may or may not seem rational, yet here we are. It's our responsibility to navigate how scarcity impacts our individual and organizational reactions.

homelessness began to project their fears onto the solution until the meeting got way out of hand. I'm being charitable here, but I think they were trying to process what would be missing for this student compared to the students living in the residence halls or off campus. To equalize these different living situations with what they could only guess was this one student's experience, administrators were ready to buy a new building to make a temporary housing service for students facing homelessness even if it would displace the current residents.

I interrupted the flowing conversation somewhere between the available cable and gym package options, reminding them that they currently had residence halls with empty rooms and could easily just set up some bunk beds in those spaces to provide temporary housing for students in need. It seemed they'd gotten distracted by equalizing a quality experience at a higher level of Maslow's hierarchy of needs instead of providing more basic needs such as a roof, bed, bathroom, and a sense of safety. I certainly wasn't trying to deny a student in need annual access to a treadmill and unlimited cable channels, but that wasn't the problem the meeting itself was called to solve. The collective fear on behalf of this student missing out on a more typical living experience for an NYU student was rooted in the individual fear of the members of the administration: being homeless.

Not knowing what the best decision is can be upsetting, to say the least, but sometimes we simply cannot know. When given a choice, we can know only some of the options we have to choose from.

Fear is the main reason my clients react too fast, do nothing for too long, or worry about being left behind. Regarding DEI initiatives, no one is leading the way, so we can't follow someone else or even be left behind — yet. We need to utilize accessible resources, time, and recognize the talents and challenges of others so that we can lead.

Second-Guessing

Many people second-guess themselves through common fears such as being found out as an impostor, looking like a fraud, or doing something embarrassing. I second-guess myself after having decided, in fear, that I made a poor decision.

The best example I can think of is a reoccurring dream I have about my parent's yearbooks. After their passing, I cleaned out my childhood home and found their high school and college yearbooks. I had no idea what to do with them, and I didn't know what they would've wanted me to do with them either. If they'd had a plan other than to stash them in the attic, I imagine they would've executed that plan before they died. To this day, I wake up in the middle of the night worried that I didn't do the right thing. I truly don't remember whether I donated them as art supplies or threw them out for recycling. I can't remember what I did, yet I fear I didn't do the right thing. As I type this, my elementary, middle, high school, and college yearbooks sit in a box because I still don't know what the "right thing" is to do. I'm paralyzed by fear about both decisions, only one of which I can do anything about now.

When my clients are in similar situations, I share a picture of my box of yearbooks. We use it as an example of something I have fearful feelings about and thus have not yet made a decision. The box represents my informed response; yes, my fears are manifested as a box full of memories that's sitting in my dining room.

Organizationally speaking, fear, especially when related to DEI initiatives, shows up in random choices that arbitrarily sprinkle resources around to a lot of different initiatives, doing none of them well and doing them at least a little. This doesn't make sense. Fear can be highly triggering by itself, but add a combination of scarcity or ambiguity and there's even more room for self-doubt. Individually and organizationally, this stalls any thoughtful response or action, which in turn results in others witnessing inaction. And that brings us to anxiety.

Anxiety

Anxiety is the itch that the other sources of fear — or triggers — don't quite scratch. In times of stress, some of the ways anxiety manifests may be totally normal, and typically we know when it isn't just stress but something bigger. My anxiety alone probably sends my therapist's extended family on vacation, yet it's my responsibility to build up familiarity with the tools needed for me to address my anxious patterns myself. Each of us must learn to recognize anxiety, both for itself and for the myriad of coping mechanisms that tame this form of fear.

Calls for austerity, fear of a recession, and similar fears can be correlated with financial forecasting or justified in some manner, but sometimes they're simply an anxious response. Anxiety often fuels our lack of interest in trying something different, listening to others who are different from us, and learning from unfamiliar situations. It can even cause us to actively lessen our outreach efforts so that we stay comfortable. I encourage you to stretch toward curiosity, innovation, and creativity. Make space for new ideas and perspectives while rewarding failures that happen along the path to successes.

Together, these five fears are examples of triggers that can happen both individually and as an organization. Let's look at another case study from one of my clients and investigate how ambiguity, scarcity, FOMO, second-guessing, and anxiety show up on an organizational level.

CHAPTER 9

Recognize "Them"

In my little town, there's an area called "Olde Town" where locally owned shops, cafés, galleries, and bars are located. A few months ago, all the streets were being repaved. I imagine the small-business owners were notified in advance and am certain they must've felt some amount of fear about how this would impact their customer traffic and sales. No one seemed to know how long the project would take, but parking was already very limited, and with the construction it would be even more so.

The levels of anxiety must've been off the charts, yet there was a solution. The store owners worked collectively to piece together staff, parking spaces, and marketing efforts to send customers to the right areas that were open. These options rotated as the project was underway, allowing all storefronts equal flow of traffic. The bonus was the development of a collaborative community. These efforts built upon an informal system the community was already using to alert each other of shoplifters passing through each location. After a week, the roads were paved, and each business owner made payroll. By deciding to serve and support one another, the community thrived through a problem they not only recognized but nimbly navigated together.

The biggest objection my clients give me regarding sharing insights across their industry smells like middle-school peer pressure to me: "It's not my fault, it's theirs!" Or better yet, "Well, they aren't doing that, so why should I?" Deciding whose responsibility it is to do or not do something is a real challenge, and it can easily cloud our ability to be objective, trust ourselves or others, and respond according to our strategic goals and stakeholder needs. I spend an extraordinary amount of time fielding questions about fixing other people or how a problem would disappear if someone else just behaved differently. Unfortunately, though this might be true, the behavior of others is out of our control and this is also true of collectives. However, if we begin to consistently claim or reclaim responsibility for our own reactions, we can respond more intentionally. Moreover, by checking our reactions we can stop projecting unmet expectations onto other organizations to perform a certain way and instead support one another. We can't reform our bullies, but we can stop being one.

Turning to COVID again for learning lessons, my Christian friends were in full panic mode as Easter 2020 approached. How could they celebrate a religious holiday full of family traditions and still meet the expectations of others? Turning to other communities of faith would've been a great idea, but it wasn't (and isn't) a habit. Jewish Purim and Passover had already occurred, with modifications for sheltering in place. Hindu and Sikh festivals were held, canceled, or turned into hybrid events. Muslims and Pagans also have important high holidays in late March to early April, not to mention all the big birthdays, weddings, graduations, and other kinds of celebrations when participants had to figure something out.

Often there are other options that could guide us, but we aren't willing to explore them. We aren't receptive to learning from others because we aren't comfortable recognizing that they might know something we don't. We don't like new things because they aren't familiar. A lack of previous experience is what makes something new, and it's exactly when we have the opportunity to learn. "Hard pass," say most of my clients.

We can't plan for everything, but we can listen and pay attention to others and learn from them. Allowing others to access a front row seat into our organized chaos so that they can learn from us instead of us pressuring each other to outperform provides relief. Being brave enough to be seen as trying to do the right thing and allowing others to guide us

We can't reform our bullies, but we can stop being one.

is challenging. However, shared recognition that the answer can only be found together is vital to solving DEI-related issues.

A perfect example of this is when I was writing a leadership curriculum for first responders, which I'd replicated from what I'd learned in my student leadership retreats. My point of contact was a retired fire chief, and we worked together to build out a multitiered international leadership retreat for high-potential EMT, fire, and police leaders. We needed a culminating decision-making activity that would really challenge the learned and ingrained thinking habits of the participants. I knew a perfect activity, and felt anxious about pitching it because this was a serious group of professionals, and I wasn't sure whether playing with blocks of wood would somehow be below them. I explained that the room would be set up with round tables and that the participants would be put into small groups. Each group would have a bag of wooden blocks as puzzle pieces and would have to race to complete a puzzle. The trick was that each table would have a piece that belonged to another table, so no one could be successful without working outside of their own table.

The chief loved it!

I'm still reflecting on the level of fear I experienced about possibly being dismissed as an expert, losing the contract, or being laughed at. Yet the idea was in fact perfect for what was necessary to teach participants to look outside of themselves for answers. It was, as the chief pointed out, an activity outside of his comfort zone that taught him the lesson: "It turns young first responders into old first responders," meaning they stay alive longer. Powerful. Looking outside of ourselves and recognizing that we both need help and can assist others is exactly how we save lives, including our own. (Insert big eye emoji here!)

This activity works as a metaphor for real life in that participants in life hear the same set of directions and pull from their own life experiences to compete in putting together a puzzle. Even with the answer provided on how to stack the wooden blocks, the first responders couldn't solve the puzzle. Rarely did anyone ever reach out to another table for assistance. More often, a teammate would make the suggestion, but would be reminded sternly that they were part of this team and that this was a competition.

Recognizing what we know is a great starting place. Then we need to ask ourselves what we don't know, because we may be missing something. DEI initiatives are exactly the same in that each organization has a set of blocks and can get only so far in their work before getting stuck. If everyone gets stuck in different places, then sharing that information could help everyone achieve their goals. Asking for help to achieve our goals isn't a sign of weakness but shows a deep commitment to do what's right, even when missing a block or two.

Before we respond, we must bridge the gap between rearranging our bag of blocks and looking around to assist others and ask them for ideas. This skill needs development, nurturing, rehearsal, and reevaluation to recognize when we and the organization are on the brink of succumbing to meaningless performance. Remember, we can't make "them" do anything; we can be responsible only for what *we* are doing to others.

There is a way through. I recommend slowing down enough to think through your own point of view, whether individually or organizationally. You may default to thinking of examples about your competitors instead, but that stems from nothing but habit. Thank you for the job security! Now try again.

I remember once when I was a kid, blowing up at my mother when she asked me to sweep the back porch. I'd just done the job the day before, and it was basically still clean. I asked her, "Why do I have to do this again? I already did it once!" She calmly responded, "So it's clean today." Like a good yoga practice, going once a year, during my lunch hour or not, is great, but to really benefit from yoga it needs to be practiced regularly. Even going as irregularly as I do, I know to listen to my body, breath, and notice where I'm either tight, balanced, blocked, or limber, and it's different every time. This is what I'm asking of you.

Develop a practice that regularly enters, exists, putters out, and restarts. The goal here is to recognize your own patterns when you're confronted with a problem you're not experiencing personally. Put differently, stumble into something you didn't know you didn't know. There, on the precipice of the unknown, what you do says a lot about your preparation and how you and your organization typically recognize what you ought to do.

When we're experiencing external pressure, we can tame our fears of ambiguity, scarcity, FOMO, second-guessing, and anxiety when we do three things:

1. Recognize we do know what we do know
2. Recognize we do know some of what we don't know
3. Recognize there is always WAY more we don't know we don't know

Take a breath, recognize what has been triggered in you or how your organization sputters into typical and comfortable action, and ask more questions first:

- Who do I compare myself to? (i.e., What is your definition of "them"?)
- Which organizations do I compare my organization to? (i.e., Identify your "them.")
- What is my intention in this moment?
- What are "they" intending to accomplish?
- What do I think I would or ought to do?
- What do I think "they" would or ought to do?
- What would happen? / What are the possible outcomes?
- How do I keep an eye on how things are going or turning out?
- How are "they" doing this?
- What might happen next?
- What could I do sooner rather than later to accommodate any of the scenarios I imagine before they happen?
- How nimble is my response process when something does happen? Can I change mid-process?
- What do "they" do to readjust? What don't they do?
- What did I learn from this process?
- What did I teach others?
- What did I learn from others' experiences?

Asking for help to achieve our goals isn't a sign of weakness but a deep and consistent commitment to do what's right.

- What did others teach someone else?

- How can I keep this learning at the top of my mind and bring it into the next experience?

- How can pressure (internal or external) inform my future decisions in both positive and negative ways?

- What patterns do I recognize from going through this experience that will help me be more prepared for whatever's next?

Wow that's a lot of questions. You need to get comfortable asking not only them but even more. I don't have the answers for you. Neither your competitors nor the go-to folks you delegate this kind of work to can answer them for you either. *You* need to do the work and ask the questions, arrive at answers, and then ask more questions. By doing so, you can lead your organization, industry, and broader community to something new and better. Someone (I'm holding a mirror up to you right now) just needs to look up from their own bag of blocks and listen for answers that haven't come to mind just yet. Remember, the goal here is to recognize something we don't even know we don't know, in ourselves, in our organizations, and in others.

It's often easier to focus on others, but I invite you to really dig deep and recognize how you and your organization respond when triggered. There are times when you're vastly prepared and others when you know you're out of your comfort zone. Hang in there and ask yourself these questions, because the answers matter:

- When do I no longer employ curiosity?

- Is there a pattern of when I show up less curious?

- When is my experience no longer useful and I just opt out?

- Do I outsource initiatives to others? Cancel them all together? Turn a blind eye? Hold my breath and hope it doesn't happen?

That last one is a hard one. Sticking your head in the sand is a common response to the unknown, but it doesn't have to be. Let's take it one step at a time.

Almost Doing Good

Someone (I'm holding a mirror up to you right now) just needs to look up from their own bag of blocks and listen for answers that haven't come to mind just yet.

Looking like an ostrich may have never crossed your mind. Maybe someone else's team is doing worse than yours, so you feel fine. This could be true and even accurate. The day will come, though, when you're going to have to justify why you were spit-polishing a landmine to begin with. The same folks you've compared yourself to will be there listening. To some degree, some of you will need to keep doing what you're doing because I have rescue dogs with sensitive stomachs, and I need to keep working to pay for their expensive dog food. Ideally, however, I'll keep working toward my own unemployment and expect you to lead. I'm holding you to a higher standard both individually and organizationally, and I expect you to do better because I recognize the potential in you. Do you?

Let's get to work.

Be Intentional

Above anything else, you must be intentional. Consider those times when you figuratively skittered out onto thin ice but hung in there, such as during natural disasters, oil crashes, housing markets tanking overnight, global pandemics, political movements, wars, and the like. You probably didn't have a binder of protocol steps to follow; you just jumped. Similarly, being intentional in your DEI-related initiatives means being conscious of the need to take a leap, perhaps even along with industries and stakeholders.

For this collaborative leap of faith to occur, you must make being intentional part of your preparatory work in developing your organizational culture. When the time comes and pressure is mounting, you can decide — as an individual and as an organization of individuals — to elevate through the unknown and support one another. To do this, you need to dust off your annual reports and really sit with what your larger intentions truly are. You must recognize the difference between your performance and your purpose.

In my MBA program, we were asked what the highest-level, most sustainable, best-for-the-planet choice any corporation could make. I answered quickly: "Close." If an organization were no longer open, it wouldn't be able to continue burning fossil fuels, creating waste, mining for resources, or potentially exploiting human labor for profit. Some argue that large corporations are the only resources flush enough to solve social problems. Others focus on the idea that the problems wouldn't exist if capitalism weren't solely profit-driven. Let's compromise and shoot for the second-best choice.

The second-best time to plant a tree is now.

Any organization can intentionally improve the world for their stakeholders. Imagine a commitment big enough that leaders like yourself joined forces to disrupt what we currently know and create something different together by recognizing, collaborating, and supporting something better.

The second-best time to plant a tree is now — there is hope!

Take Responsibility

My clients squirm in their boardroom chairs when I challenge them to take responsibility for deciding, at best, what the second-best answer is for the most sustainable action for the planet. Closing their business is generally unanimously seen as not an option, but significant changes like this do happen to keep up with technology. Remember when we had a gizmo on our dashboards that gave us directions? Some laggards still print out directions or use paper maps to navigate their way around. I grew up riding in the passenger seat of my father's delivery truck while reading a Mapsco. I had to Google the mapping company to see whether it's still in business, and it seems it collapsed in 2022 when no one stepped up to buy it.

Sweeping change isn't new to any organization, and though leadership teams can often see it coming, not all pivot fast enough or at all. Garmin, for example, lost a ton of revenue from its automotive and mobile streams, but the company has garnered huge gains by using the same technology for outdoor and fitness tracking, something that smart phone users weren't doing (yet).

Making decisions is hard. We have to balance risk with reward, and we have only short-term and long-term forecasting to use as information for venturing a guess. Mapsco likely didn't plan for its swift closure, and Garmin likely didn't know that evolving technology would lessen the demand for driving direction gizmos. Garmin may have had an easier decision of doubling down on its corner of the technology market; instead of accepting that its technology was obsolete, it reconfigured its business model to focus on outdoor activity mapping, leading to a steady revenue stream.

Diversifying revenue streams and pivoting based on market demand are considerations that need to be at the table when discussing the unknown future. Change is possible, but you and your organization likely won't achieve it until you have to, at least not without some preparatory forecasting. If you can make informed guesses, you can claim responsibility for your thought processes while also being crystal clear of your intentions and your stakeholder expectations. You can even leave space for change as you learn.

CHAPTER 10

Bridge the Gap through Better Connections

Because we recognize that change is inevitable, a business case can generally be made for ensuring the ability to adapt. Even as individuals, we often have very challenging conversations, some of which go off the rails, yet we're still able to hang in there because the topic, context, or person is important to us. Then there are the times when we do nothing. We opt out. Nah. I challenge us (myself included) to recognize the patterns of when we opt out, because we can learn from these habits. Furthermore, we can learn from someone who may be unable to uphold a commitment by being more understanding and supportive.

Conversations that matter come not from a self-serving place but from a higher standard or an expectation of doing better for the benefit of all. Let's take this one step at a time, beginning with a model I like to refer to as "Better Connections."

The Better Connections model is rooted in leaving each moment better than it was. A well-known example is leaving a campsite in better condition than when you arrived. Sure, when you pulled in that wasn't your trash, and now it isn't someone else's trash to deal with either.

Likewise, you can learn to recognize a new role that your organization could play across your industry and surrounding community, one that impacts the lives of your stakeholders in ways you have yet to discover. You just have to start by recognizing that there's more you don't know that you don't know, get comfortable with this reality, and work with the resources you do know about. You can host intentional conversations, deploy product lines, or support large-scale initiatives that align with your intentions, even when you learn that you've missed the mark. You can keep your word, align your intentions with your actions, recognize when there's a misalignment, and expect others to do the same.

When you've done your preparatory work, making this kind of commitment is in direct alignment with your organization's beliefs and values. Your stakeholders will be able to identify this commitment in all that you do, both internally and externally in the community, so intentionally making better connections is congruent with what you ought to already be doing. Recognize the difference and do something about it now. How? Let's find out.

Listen to Others as If They Are Wise

I once got a fortune cookie with a slip of paper inside that read, "Listen to others as if they are wise." It didn't make sense to me. Then, one day, I was on a walk with a dear friend's young son, Neil. They live in a rural area of Vermont, and we walked for about an hour or so deep into a forested area that didn't seem to follow a trail of any kind. Neil delighted in showing me fiddleheads, edible berries, different types of tree leaves, bugs, and other evidence of nature.

At some point, I got worried that we were lost and that it would be dark before we got back to the house. I don't see well at night and don't like being lost, so as the dusk insects increased their presence, my anxiety

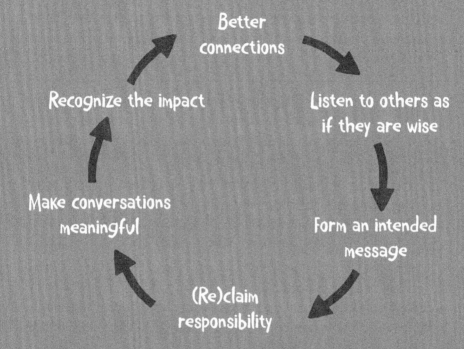

increased as well. A number of times, I mentioned to Neil that I was getting worried about being too far away from home. Once he noticed that I really needed to get home, he took off running. I panicked and ran after him.

We ran maybe one hundred yards before we were back at the house. Turned out we'd been walking in a circular pattern and had never gotten far from home. I should mention that Neil has done this walk every day of his life. I hadn't trusted him. I hadn't listened to him as if he had any information that I did not. I was lost. He was right at home.

What Neil taught me that day is the importance of making better connections. To truly do so, I have to employ my whole self so that I can show up not just as a listener but as a genuinely curious, authentic, generous, and vulnerable person. By not focusing on the transcript or what's being said, I can forget the words and focus on the authenticity of the moment. While I was focusing on the experience of being lost in the woods of Vermont in the dark, I missed moments of sheer glee that I could've shared with Neil if I'd only trusted him.

Sure, it would be fun to monitor, tattle tale, and call out others for their missteps, mistakes, or misalignments, but the truth is that we each have enough work to do on our own. Industry-specific environmental, social, and governance standards exist to monitor a collective agreement when managing risks, strategic planning, and growth opportunities. It's up to us and our organizations to abide by these standards, report honestly, and allow for learning curves to become public. We don't really do this, however, because we succumb to our habits when trying to outperform one another.

What if part of our monitoring processes involved being curious enough to learn from others and share our own vulnerabilities? Ignoring whatever feathers I just ruffled on your and your organization's neck, I invite you to take a moment and recognize what just came up for you. It will shine a light on the cultural experience of your organization that you may or may not be conscious of in the first place. The answers you're looking for may be with "them." You just need to listen.

Are you familiar with your inside voice? I like to joke that if you answered that question, it was likely not out loud; you used an inner voice. We do this all the time. This inside voice is imperative to acknowledge within us because it's with this voice that we make all judgments and assumptions that then inform our behaviors.

In the woods with Neil that day, my demeanor shifted whether I meant it to happen or not. I'm certain I reentered his home acting like a self-deprecating little girl. This is the difference between intent and impact. I did not intend to freak out nor validate a theory Neil was forming about adult behavior. I wanted to get home before dark and did not trust Neil to take care of me, and that impacted our ability to connect.

Recognizing intent and impact isn't complicated, but it can be difficult. And finding the solution isn't easy, but the solution itself is simple. For better connections to happen, we need to converse with curiosity by listening from the inside out. When I was with Neil, my internal voice was having its own conversation. I was desperate to know how far we were from the house and started feeling panicked and frustrated that I'd set myself up to be reliant on an eight-year-old. These fears then sent me directly to my self-limiting beliefs, and I found myself entering an internal conversation about why I always fail to plan ahead, all while completely missing yet another of the world's precious and magical gifts of a found animal track. Two different conversations were taking place: 1) my fears were telling me that I couldn't truly trust a young boy's discoveries or nature lessons, and 2) I found myself in a self-talk spiral of a little girl who should've known better. Curiously, I wondered what impact my internal voice had on the little boy's excursion.

After I calmed down a bit, I told Neil how I doubted his sense of direction and asked him what it was like for him. He quickly responded, "Adults are weird and worry instead of wonder."

Successful connections and built relationships cannot alone be a foundation. I am responsible for how this foundation aligns with my own values, ideas, and interactions with others. It's my responsibility to develop a conscious habit at my foundation to foster more successful relationships.

Our lived experiences can directly impact our ability to listen, form messages, make meaning, and truly connect with one another. We can use this bias, whether positive or negative, to intentionally make better connections. We just have to try. We also need to make a conscious note of the differences and similarities between and among the lived experiences of Person A and Person B. Whether good or bad, our experiences inform our choices and our capacity to connect with another person deeply and genuinely. This applies to organizations as well because stakeholders are watching us and comparing the choices we make to their other options in the marketplace.

A prime example of a well-intentioned use of our limiting habits that exemplifies how better connections are made occurred upon my last visit to see Neil, who, by the way, is now in his early 20s and is a volunteer firefighter in rural Vermont. (Of course he is!) During my visit, he and his mother, a longtime friend, were joking about how when Neil was growing up she'd kept pressuring him to be a sweeper (I think it was called a sweeper, or is that a quidditch position?), an aggressive defensive position that runs a soccer field. My friend was a competitive soccer player and coach, and while we served in the Peace Corps together, she even organized a soccer league in her town of service. Neil shared how he was a terrible sweeper and that being terrible made him almost hate the sport. He worried about disappointing his mother and felt pressure to extend the family legacy, but he wasn't very good. Then, one day, he substituted for the goalie during practice and played great defense. Who knew that a super-fast international soccer player would raise an avid woodsman *and* competitive goalie?

Imagining this conversation in real time, these intentional spaces full of curiosity make more sense, don't they? Intentionally providing space for a better connection allows for both you and the other person in the conversation to show up fully. You can choose to see them as "differently right" and leave room for edits. You can take each connection and move one step closer to internally processing the exchange so that you can better connect with yourself and others. This is easier to type than to do,

For better connections
to happen, we need to
converse with curiosity by
listening from the inside out.

but who else can slow down your mind enough to try? To better connect, you must listen to your inner voice *and* others as if they are wise.

Before moving on, take a second and notice that it may feel like you haven't done anything yet. But that isn't true. Any preparatory work typically goes unacknowledged when we're in a high-stakes situation. Then there's the work it takes to realign, assess, and decide to recognize the current situation we're feeling as an individual, organization, and industry. Put yourself in your stakeholders' shoes. Take a step, imagine you're your immediate competitor, ask yourself what they would want or need in this situation, then choose to be that resource for them. Break the cycle of siloing that applies too much pressure on leaders to know everything and instead allow yourself some space to recognize you now know something you didn't know before. Then you can create space to determine what you would've done and what others have or could do so that you can make an informed response instead of just reacting out of habit.

Remember, there's likely another option that you just aren't seeing. That doesn't mean you're doing anything wrong, just that you could be doing it better. I remember a TikTok trend a few summers ago of dogs participating in a magic trick. The dog is shown two upside-down cups, and one is lifted to show the dog some treats. Both cups are then slid around the tabletop in different directions before the dog chooses one. The cup of choice is lifted, and the dog treats are revealed and quickly eaten. Victory! Then the second cup is lifted to reveal a lot more dog treats. The dog followed the typical directions and picked the first cup. In the video trend, there was a consistent look of confusion on the dogs' faces when they saw a different option than the one they'd expected. They looked disappointed in themselves for not knowing what was in the other cup and shocked at their parent for tricking them.

Whatever you're choosing to do, take a second to think about alternative options. I challenge you to recognize that you did as expected *and* that there could also be another option that's even better. Question your choice, and if it still stands, your confidence in that choice will increase. Then share this process with everyone openly.

I bet that made the hairs on your organization's neck stand on end!

Form an Intended Message

To respond instead of to react means to slow down the process enough to review past answers and ask more questions. Before we deploy "best practices," we need to take a second to intentionally decide on a plan of action. Once we determine that, we can consciously respond.

First we must recognize our lack of habits. We need to examine what we're able to do — our known knowns and our known unknowns — and leave room for everything else. By intentionally choosing a message that aligns with your organization's culture, you'll respond more confidently in your own voice and not out of performance. Moreover, you won't do something that's so out of alignment that it causes more problems.

There's a fine balance between forming a message and being clear on the intended meaning of the message. Let's explore this.

We get to choose what kind of message we want to send as much as we get to choose how we're going to receive a message. The manner in which we communicate is deeply rooted in our habitual behavior patterns. (SPOILER ALERT: our patterns are on both the individual, organizational, and industry levels.) For example, I recently shared a picture via text message with my dear friend Sylvie. In response, I received this text: "I think you have the wrong number." The name that accompanied the phone number was "Sylvia." I did a double take because the only Sylvia I know is my Aunt Sylvia, who passed away a few years ago. My first response was to question why this stranger had my aunt's cell phone. I took a minute before responding, then realized that Sylvia's number must've been recycled after she'd passed. I also realized that I'd selected "Sylvia" instead of "Sylvie" when I'd sent the picture.

I responded to the person with my aunt's former number, "Sorry for my mistake. I meant this for someone else. You have my aunt's cell number. She was a wonderful person. I bet you are too." They responded by saying they loved the idea of having a cell number with a positive history and that they were available if I ever just needed to text my aunt.

In that moment, I chose to reform my response, and it resulted in a better connection. Following all the communication training I've gone through, I made sure that I used positive "I" messages that didn't blame the other person for not knowing they had my aunt's number. I relaxed my shoulders, shifted the tone of my voice (even if it was just inside my own head), and typed a text with the intention of having a better connection rather than just admitting to a mistake. Then I resent the picture to my Sylvie.

By intentionally forming a better message, I made at least four better connections:

1. To my Aunt Sylvia and my memory of our relationship
2. To my friend Sylvie who loved the story about the stranger
3. To the stranger who may not have known the history of their cell number
4. To you, the reader, because you may share this story

Forming a message with your full self in mind matters. To allow space for others to fully show up, you must allow space for *your* full self to show up. This means that the good, bad, ugly, and awesome parts of you are just as important as the elements of the person you want to connect with.

Consider how often crisis response protocols are created through a cumbersome process that results in a less than positive reaction. Organizations often quickly form media campaigns, slogans, and names for new products that ride pop culture trends, slang, or other temporal virtue signals. In the time it takes to complete a roll out, the organization's message misses the mark. An organization can look like it's trying, but if it's too late in its response, the effort can look artificial and manipulative instead of providing intentional alignment. This is where our intentions come in while forming the message implied in our response.

Pay attention and notice your own meanings as they inform the intention behind your messages. Do not passively listen, but engage, ask questions, and leave room for others to share and connect with you too. Your self-awareness will role model the space for the other person to share from an authentic place. Being curious with your intentions and exchanging messages in a generous manner will not eradicate miscommunication, misunderstanding, and disagreement, but it will keep these elements from stifling or destroying your connections as well as increase your opportunities to make better ones.

Give yourself a break. As you enter a challenging conversation or turn to a contentious relationship or high-stakes campaign launch, step into the connection with the future in mind. What might be going on with *them*, the "outsiders"? What are some potential reactions? Try hard to not direct or set them up for a particular response. Having fewer expectations for the outcome of the connection or the other person's role in a conversation allows you to remain focused on yourself and how you show up in the moment.

We are never entitled to a response or an engagement. We do, however, get to protect ourselves, feel safe, lean on others for help, and process with others. We are responsible for the patterns or ingredients that develop into our feelings of danger. Once we become aware of where these feelings come from, we decide intentionally whether we want to keep this response pattern or change it. Regardless, our authentic purpose is to reflect on our interactions to inform our next connection opportunity.

My therapist once told me, "The hardest thing to do is to let someone be wrong about you." Man, that still burns. And it's so accurate. I'm not entitled to an accurate portrayal in other people's minds. Instead of using my energy to prove myself to them, what I can do is reflect on why I am the way I am. And if it's congruent with my beliefs and values, then I can proceed as I am more confidently. Still, this doesn't mean that it doesn't hurt when others are wrong about me.

When you have to make organizational decisions, hopefully they'll align with your experienced cultural foundation. Even if they're not broadly understood, your stakeholders will value your consistency in upholding your beliefs and values, and that emboldens loyalty. This exchange allows you to share your views and feelings, as well as your lived experiences, with others so that they have a chance to connect and share their authentic stories with you. Listening generously to them while they share their stories creates more opportunities to powerfully connect, which increases the amount of support each party feels and leads to deeper connections. It builds fertile ground for creativity, innovation, and teamwork.

I explained this once to a client using their organization's newly adopted marketing plan as a metaphor. The organization had spent a lot of money on a new marketing strategy that came with a branding kit of specific fonts, colors, tag lines, and logos they planned to use consistently. Once the leaders of this organization adopted and deployed this strategy, they were able to make decisions much more easily.

Once you know the boundaries, you have a lot of freedom. I encourage you and your leadership team to go back to the preparatory work and understand the culture your organization is aspiring to operate under. It will make forming messages and responses much easier. By knowing why your organization exists and how it's in true alignment with your stakeholders, you'll not only be able to make more informed responses but will elevate, if not pressure, your industry partners to do the same.

(Re)Claim Responsibility

A couple of years ago, I was in a pretty serious car accident while driving my Fiat home from the library. A neighborhood intersection near my home has a stop sign, and I had the right of way as a car ran through at 80 miles an hour. (A quick PSA here: if you haven't been in a car accident with airbags, I highly recommend it!) The car clipped my front bumper, sending my Fiat spinning around the corner. After the airbags deflated, there was powder everywhere.

Meanwhile, I was still trying to figure out what had happened. My phone and library book were on the floorboard, and oddly the rest of my keys had separated from the ignition key because of the force of impact. The first thing I remember is a homeless man digging through my glove box while telling me my car was on fire. I slowly realized that the airbag powder looked like smoke to him, and I calmly told him that I was fine and that nothing was on fire. I then asked him to get out of my car before thinking, *Am I alright? It doesn't seem like anything's on fire. I should call Loren, insurance, the police.* Though I tend to be pretty calm in a crisis, I realized that if I'd been half a second earlier, the car would've hit my driver's door and this would've been a very different situation.

Enough dust settled that I found my phone, and as I called Loren I could see three barefoot children piling out of the other car. I didn't see any evidence of seatbelts or car seats. I was clearly not at fault, and in this moment I had a choice: I could decide who I was going to be when I got out of what was left of my car.

With gratitude for being seemingly fine, having full insurance coverage, and with relief that nothing was on fire, I turned my full attention to the other car. I decided in that moment who and how I was going to be with the other driver. Rather than assume any blame, I claimed my responsibility to have a better conversation with another driver, who likely had more at stake than I did. I decided that no matter what unfolded, I'd be 100 percent responsible for the impact of my connection with her. Centering a desire to have a better connection allowed me to take a moment to observe the situation from an outside perspective so that I could remain clear on my intentions. By intentionally forming my thoughts, I could engage with her without being defensive or fearful.

Taking responsibility is different from accepting fault or blame. Utilizing our organizational culture and industry partners' responses to various situations may seem like a high-stakes venture, but it simply comes down to being responsible for our own impact. One of the biggest unknowns is the impact we have on others. Occasionally we get to learn of our impact on someone or a situation, and we should look at these moments as true gifts.

The key to taking responsibility is to be crystal clear on our motivations and intentions prior to rolling out a message. That way, we can claim responsibility for our choices even when something unintentional results. We need to know why we're making the choices we're making and be able to back them up with our proven priorities, beliefs, and values. It's highly likely that something is happening that you won't know about until it's so pervasive that you experience pressure to do something about it. It's then that you'll look back on your decision-making process and recognize whether you reacted or gave an informed response.

Though intentionally making better connections is super simple, it isn't always easy. Nor is (re)claiming responsibility for only the impacts we can control. Our actions must support our connections. Remember, we can all be differently right. If in the moment we can suspend our final drafts, we can leave room for a truthful exchange and focus on learning about each other. By holding genuine curiosity with generous advocacy, we can support our dialogue intentionally, whether we're at the car wash, a grocery store, dinner table, or the board table.

Missed connections happen when we don't show up to a conversation authentically. We cannot pretend that pieces of our lived experiences don't show up or are resolved. We carry our histories with us in every conversation, and they lay the foundation of all our connections.

Making better connections with others is only half of the work of taking responsibility. You also need to look inward and become more self-aware. In connecting with your habitual behavior patterns and having a more truthful sense of yourself, you can discover, or perhaps uncover, that you are truly enough as is. Focus on doing the best you can with what you have some of the time. I promise it's better than nothing, and what you bring to these connections, conversations, and interactions is enough.

Making promises to others of real change is one battle I consistently grapple with, and keeping promises I've made to myself often starts a war among all my habits, self-limiting beliefs, and excuses. When I first started my business, I had to have a tough conversation with myself when I started gaining corporate clients. I had to ask myself, *Are there clients I wouldn't work with because of their choices?* Some corporations are responsible for environmental degradation, human exploitation, bad politics, and even war, death, disease, and greed. I had to sit with myself and dig into my own beliefs and values system to determine what kind of organization I wanted to be. If I stripped away the branding, logos, charm, and humor, what would my business represent that is true to why I started it in the first place? Has this foundation changed over time?

The key to taking
responsibility is to
be crystal clear on
our motivations and
intentions prior to
rolling out a message.

What I determined is that I believe these three things deeply:

1. Everyone deserves a place where they feel seen — no matter where they work

2. Doing the right thing is always the right thing to do

3. As Marcus Aurelius and my husband like to say, "If it isn't true, don't say it, and if it isn't right, don't do it.

I can make organizational decisions with these foundational values at the center and be 100 percent responsible for wherever they take me. Sure, I've made some mistakes, but these foundational values have steered me through them. Moreover, they've guided me to the right clients for more than two decades.

Make Conversations Meaningful

Back to my car accident. Loren and I were sitting on the curb across the street as the other driver returned to her car after getting my contact information. The police had gone, and all that was left of the accident was glass on the road that the tow truck driver didn't sweep up. The other driver approached me with an authoritarian attitude that may have just come with the clipboard she was carrying. Though she was clearly at fault, she wasn't interested in conversation or small talk. Instead of getting defensive, I couldn't help but imagine how scared she must be in that moment. I am responsible for who and how I show up and ideally the choices I make align with who and how I want to be in the world.

I watched her family drive away in a mostly unscathed car and tried to understand the difference between visible damage and internal damage. The metaphor is not lost on me here.

When the insurance company called me a few days later, I asked about her and her kids to make sure they weren't injured. I was relieved to hear they were fine.

We get chances like this to make meaning from moments. Don't waste them.

Just when you may be getting uncomfortable, relax. No one is good at this. Recognizing a high-stakes situation is hard, and responding to one is even harder. Do the work to recognize when you and your organization are good and bad at this. Like a yoga practice, this is ongoing, forever work. At times you'll excel, at others you'll lick your wounds, and many other times you won't even notice the difference. Building up the ability to recognize a problem you may not experience firsthand is what leadership requires, and most of my clients haven't acknowledged the need to do the right thing, let alone as big a thing as trying to get DEI initiatives right.

And yet, here you are, still reading.

I find that my clients are still hanging onto their uncomfortable conversations because, ultimately, the answers are within their own leadership desires. Progress is just about having the confidence to voice their own limitations, vulnerabilities, and uncertainties while being curious and generous in building something forward together in an authentic manner that aligns with the organization's ideal culture. Easier said than done. Luckily, we already have a habit of reacting, so let's use this often-misguided habit for good.

Most diversity experts state that people are never supposed to make judgments and assumptions. I disagree. I think we make assumptions to feel safe and prepared, and therefore we can make meaning of them. Full disclosure, this meaning isn't always accurate, but we don't need to stop the practice just because something's inaccurate. Feeling safe and prepared is likely the only way we'd show up in the first place. Only then can we build the habit of leaving room for edits and becoming more accurate by adjusting the story we made up in the first place.

Making judgments as unknowns that become knowns is already a business curiosity practice. We make uncertain decisions when forecasting or making educated guesses, and we formulate our organizations' strategic plans. Let's just use the same tools when we learn of something we didn't know we didn't know and adjust accordingly so that we can keep showing up — or at least recognize when we aren't willing to and figure out why.

Clarity is required to form a message in the first place, but in claiming our own sense of responsibility we often forget that. We must be clear about what we do with the process of making meaning as well. We might receive only a small portion of the messages in the manner in which they were intended, and these messages could be observed, picked up secondhand, or delivered in a direct conversation. It's up to us to take in these messages as they were intended and to notice the patterns of our responses as we make meaning from the impact the message has on others. If not us, then who?

It's way more habitual to offset or outsource responsibility to our competitors, the federal government, or the supreme court. I'm asking you to attempt to be 100 percent responsible for your responses and to notice when you aren't. Often, others will try to highlight for us patterns of behavior that we don't even notice. We get feedback all the time, and any meaning we make of it typically comes from a place of defensiveness or is deflected back to the sender of the message. When we create a safe space based on curiosity, vulnerability, generosity, and authenticity, we build trust, and better discussions can begin to regularly occur without a facilitator. If we give new ideas space to develop, our conversations can grow and include more people while also having a structure for the discussions so that we can stay grounded as well as focused on the topic at hand.

Listening to ourselves and to the feedback, stories, and experiences of others is key to getting around our go-to excuses. To listen, we need to stop talking. We must take in the messages around us and stop voicing our opinions both inside and outside of our heads. We need to look for patterns, nonverbal messages, validation, and contradictions from others and watch the flow of our conversations.

Being open to an unscripted conversation allows you to engage in a whole new way. You may feel overwhelmed at first, so tell one person and get help. Ask them to pay attention to how you show up in conversations. How does your body language change? What about the rate of your speech? Your tone? Do you interrupt? Where is your eye contact? Does the way you listen shift? Take their feedback as helpful no matter what patterns they notice.

Our lived experiences, self-reflections, and development of our self-awareness fuel the exchange of histories with one another. Everything about who, how, and where we are and who, how, and where we've been passes between each person we choose to engage with, and even those we don't.

It takes practice, patience, and courage to hold responsibility for our own biases, empathy for our own and others' histories, and a genuine sense of virtue in our conversations.

Recognize the Impact

"Wait. I have to be courageous too?" the lead partner in a global law firm let slip out. His typically well-paced and tempered wording changed tempo because he thought he was finished.

We were at a high-end French restaurant where I'd politely asked for the chef's choice, a trick I learned about from a chef girlfriend when you don't understand what's on the menu. We were all a little out of our comfort zones. I was grateful that the waiter kept changing out my flatware to go with each course and that my client's legal counsel seemed to appreciate my not judging him for his misstep regarding his firm's diversity initiatives.

I was listening and asking questions about what he was sharing so he wouldn't feel judged. My inside voice was fascinated that he really thought he'd mastered and completed his DEI work. He was sharing, maybe even bragging about, how his law firm had a long history of hiring from a pool of interns selected between their first and second years at Ivy League Law Schools and therefore didn't have a diversity issue. (The first summer of law school hasn't weeded out all the misfits yet, or so I learned from his summary of their DEI protocol.)

I asked him how his firm encouraged similar firms to include equivalent programs. He looked at me like I was crazy and began explaining to me how powerful and financially lucrative his firm was, with billions of dollars negotiated under its leadership. I didn't say anything.

Let me be clear here. I could've launched into the history of higher education in the US, touching on state schools, Historically Black Colleges and Universities (HBCUs), and how selecting from only top-tier universities prequalified his misfits in a way that negated a successful inclusion program. Instead, I listened. I listened like I didn't know his answers because I didn't.

He continued on about being a maverick by purposefully seeking out what I would call nontraditional students with varied professional backgrounds because of their bravery to pivot from education to the military to law, or something of the sort. It is possible that this practice does in fact what it is intended to accomplish and there are other ways to do the same. I suggest to clients that they decide, take responsibility for their choices, and then they will be prepared for what will follow.

I hear over and over again that I'm perceived to be fearless. I habitually deflect these comments, largely because I'm anxious and so debilitated by my own fears that I can't easily understand how I could be brave or courageous. Over time, I've come to terms with the fact that when I fear something, I usually forge ahead and try anyway (even if shaking in cute shoes). Often the reward or goal outweighs the risk or cost of the very thing that's causing my fear, so I step forward. This act has become a pattern in my life and is now a habit. Courage to be all my imperfect self as often as possible is brave because it comes with risk and at the cost of feeling insecure or like I'm a failure and need to be reprimanded. The reward is being true to myself while (re)claiming responsibility for all that's in my control.

With every conversation, we have the opportunity to make a better connection. And the impact we have on a connection is all we have to really make better ones. When thinking about conversations that are often contentious or fearful, we can start by looking at our lived experiences, then leave space for someone else to have a very different experience than we might've assumed. To be open to accepting that our message may have an unintended impact, we must stay focused and be clear on what we're trying to say.

Better connections come from sticking to the subject at hand and not bringing in other variables or distractions. Having a "broad scope" conversation can lead to a pileup effect that becomes a challenge to engage with or respond to. To make the best connection with another person, we need to form a message focused on one clear element and present that in conversation. Of course, other factors may be contributing to the problem under discussion, but even that can lead to richer connections. Being open to these richer connections allows others to share and you to ask questions about their experiences. Paired with your questions and those of others, these opportunities add value to every connection. Every lived experience is authentic, even the ones we don't like.

Another way we can positively impact our connections is through having a clearer understanding of the vocabulary, acronyms, variables, symbols, and systems that are connected to the topic at hand. Being open to new, shared, and differing uses of terminology allows for all conversation partners to teach and learn from one another for as long as each partner wishes to participate.

In following the Better Connections model, there's no guaranteed closure and no declared winner in a conversation, nor does every conversation have a set start, middle, or end. A better connection can pick up, pause, and pick back up again without a clear end.

When receiving feedback or engaging in making a better connection, be mindful of how your own lived experiences and behavioral patterns show up in conversation regardless of the others involved. Taking responsibility for these patterns is truly the most generous response you can have when someone is being vulnerable with you because it allows you to return the favor and accept their truth for the gift that it is. There's no better connection than that.

Use Long Spoons to Feed Others

My paternal grandfather told me a story once that involved long spoons. I never knew if he made up these stories, so you may be familiar with this one. The idea is that there's plenty of food to be had, but the utensils are too heavy and long to be used individually. Some groups will get angry and frustrated and starve to death. Get out of these groups. Other groups will use the tools they have by asking for help from others to lift the heavy spoons and work together to feed another group member on the other side of the table, then rotate so that all pitch in and thrive. Build something better with these groups. The idea that one could just slurp out of their own bowl never occurs in the story, but I see it in my work. Teams inside of a single organization don't share information with one another, let alone other teams — departments — or competitors! Others maybe just sulk or complain or demand the right tools as if the circumstances are a trick and the solution an entitlement. The solution I am suggesting here, especially in regard to DEI initiatives is you need all of the members of your team and the others on your "them" team to get everyone fed. Working together you can lift the tools you have to benefit others that in turn can do the same for you. Individually, organizationally, and across your own industry, you can benefit from helping, sharing, giving, and supporting others who in turn will do the same.

At a recent speaking engagement, an audience member asked, "If I want to connect with someone but they have not heard your keynote about holding space, won't it be weird?" I responded that entering a conversation with a brochure of definitions and connection models would be weirder. With each conversation attempt, with ourselves and with others, we must enter a connection with a sense of curiosity and ask genuine questions in anticipation of learning something. We must listen to the other person as if they are wise and try to learn something from them. When we hold that space, we avoid having expectations for the outcome. This is a good kind of weird because it leaves us open to holding a conversation without sacrificing a piece of ourselves.

My paternal grandfather told me a story once that involved long spoons. The idea is that there's plenty of food to be had, but the utensils are too heavy and long to be used individually.

On a recent webinar, a participant privately messaged me, "Sometimes I want to talk about what I'm learning, but I'm so afraid I'm going to offend someone or sound like a moron in the process, and it seems like I should not be talking about it because it's not about business. How do I do this?" I read the chat message aloud during the Q&A because I thought it was an important reality to talk about. This person remained anonymous, and their coworkers came off mute to agree with the sentiment. I then shared that when learning something new, it is new. A learning environment is supported by meeting questions where they're originating from and then truly listening for growth and next steps. This type of learning environment takes someone through a process that at the end has the prize of not just a newly acquired skill or idea but the experience of learning. After I explained this, the same participant chatted to me privately again, saying, "Thank you for your response. I am almost in tears." Frankly, I was too.

Ideally, we need to actively embrace our inner conversations to unlock the patterns of our behavior. Only once we recognize how we show up can we decide what we want to keep and what we want to change. A genuine sense of curiosity, generosity, authenticity, and vulnerability can lead to significantly more powerful conversations, with others as well as with ourselves.

I do feel the need to remind you that we're shooting to do the best we can some of the time with what we already have. Remember, this is not a model of explicit answers. Far too often, I see folks who wield models, knowledge, and vocabulary like weapons when they're in conversations with others. This is not a call for more cape-bearers and sword-carriers. I do not present this information as a tool for "gotcha moments" that you can use to attack someone else or to discipline yourself for unsavory behaviors. This Do-Good Triangle model is both simple and complex. We are all a part of this complicated system, and the art of conversation — listening to connect, sharing to relate, and (re)claiming responsibility — is the antidote.

What does it mean to be "good enough now"? It's unrealistic to live my life or hold every conversation as though I were having my last discussion with every living being I know. Sometimes I don't want to talk at all. Other times I'm excellent at it, but this excellence may be self-serving or for someone else. One of my favorite quotes by none other than Dolly Parton herself is, "If you see someone without a smile, give 'em yours!"

If I were to orchestrate my moments of excellence and keep track of them on a scorecard, I'd miss all the excellent moments I could share with others. This is why a paradigm shift is required to change our habits so that the intended and unintended impacts of our behavior patterns can truly be a reflection of our whole selves whether we are conscious of them or not.

The truth is that we need strategists, activists, and passionate people to collaborate even if at first glance they seem to be on opposite sides of an issue. What we're currently doing isn't increasing the amount of joy anyone is experiencing. Some of the wealthiest members of our society seem miserable, and increasingly more children are suffering from hunger, poor education, and a lack of stability at home. Even animals are suffering from weather and traffic changes that make it harder for them to thrive. You know what always works to lessen the suffering? The same thing I've been saying all along: doing the best we can with what we have some of the time. Your organization has resources that can serve your stakeholders in ways others can't. If you all were to share your resources, everyone would benefit.

What if real, lasting change cost nothing and required nothing new? It seems trying for that would be worth a shot. After a decade or so of educating and training myself and others, I've found that in my own life, the simple act of looking inward instead of outward for an answer that can be developed, created, bought, or built just works better. Perhaps the cost of doing so is higher because looking inward is rooted in self-awareness and taking responsibility for problems that affect others. Just because something isn't a problem for you doesn't mean it isn't a problem. Perhaps that's the highest cost of all: a lack of real connection through really listening to ourselves and others.

Can you speak up and use your leadership position to bring up a novel idea in a group that's complaining about how heavy and long their spoons are? Can you share your wooden blocks with others? Again, it seems worth a shot.

If we can move forward acknowledging that a difficult topic or complex problem needs to be resolved — in our relationships, at work, or in the world — we can see that it ultimately comes down to a simple problem of perspective. The longer we keep pointing a finger away from us, the longer the problem lies outside us. What if this is the paradigm shift required for real and lasting change? I'm not suggesting that all problems lie within us, but perhaps the answers do.

Paying attention even to seemingly little things, such as your stance when you get defensive, is important to helping feed others. When do you become defensive? Is there a pattern? When are you less likely to get defensive even if the ingredients are there? When does it seem to be more or less challenging to listen and take in new information? Ask yourself the same questions when you think about when you do or don't intervene, procrastinate or initiate, and make excuses or try. Each of us must acknowledge that our lived experiences make us who and how we are in this life.

Cultivating self-interest is dangerously close to being self-absorbed. I'd venture a guess that these skill sets are in the same grocery aisle, yet they're very different from one another. Being self-absorbed in the day and age of selfies, instant gratification, and immediacy is a statement of our lack of connection with one another. I was recently in Jamaica for a service trip and engaged with another volunteer about why she took so many pictures. She was just as curious why I did not. I don't bring my phone because I want to be present, and she takes pictures to remember. I'm not sure whether either approach is ideal, but neither is self-absorbed. Both parties held their sense of self at the center of the conversation, but each with a different intent. Neither of us is "righter" or "wronger" than the other.

To be an ally is to understand our realm of influence and how we came about, using the access that we, in fact, already have. Again, this isn't a one-time process but a lifelong process of (re)reclaiming responsibility,

The longer we keep
pointing a finger away
from us, the longer the
problem lies outside us.

gaining awareness, and being open to new experiences and lessons shared by others.

So let's put this into action. Let's pretend you and your organization have an aligned understanding of your organizational culture and have full and open support of a preparatory dialogue across all corners of your value chain. You have the clarity necessary to recognize the role fear is playing on you, your team, the organization, your stakeholders, and the industry. This foundation of responsibility is motivating your organization to elevate your industry to do the best it can with what it has some of the time while also claiming 100 percent responsibility for its choices. This is a big ask, and honestly I don't know anyone who's come close to this, but let's pretend and apply this new cyclical approach to a big movement that most of my clients got -*so close* to getting almost right.

#BLM

The #BlackLivesMatter (#BLM) movement started in 2013 in direct response to exponentially higher rates of violence toward Black women, men, and children at the hands of police and first responders. It surfaced again in 2020 after the murder of George Floyd swept US-based mainstream media. Soon after, organizations and companies felt they had to have some sort of public #BLM statement on their websites or public-facing marketing materials, even if they had no DEI strategic plan in place. The plan was not their focus—it was the statement.

There was (and will likely continue to be) a struggle to say the right thing even when there was no internal consensus on a statement or the motivation to have one. These types of statements can become tokenizing and hypocritical, and when written out of fear they can not only be misaligned with the #BLM mission but cause harm.

Not having a statement also sends a message that may or may not be intended. Though organizational leaders felt pressure to say something, they worried about saying the wrong thing and didn't know what the right thing to say was. There was no template of what a #BLM statement should say nor a mandate that every organization should have one posted. This would've negated the organizational reflection required to acknowledge intuitional and systemic racism in the first place. When a full commitment in support of #BLM wasn't an option but pressure was mounting, many organizations compromised with "non-statements," such as placeholders for the best response. Instead of risking saying the wrong thing, and with no examples of the best thing, non-statements acknowledged only the need for a stated response to a vague reference of #BLM. It was as if these organizations were trying to explain why they didn't have a formal response and justifying their decision as distinctive from those of organizations that had no statement at all.

I worked with a company several years ago that wanted to hang up a giant Black Lives Matter banner to show support. The leaders had internal discussions and worried they might be criticized for not doing it sooner. Then they worried they'd be criticized for not also hanging a progressive flag (such as for LGBTQ+ communities) nor including other marginalized communities. They received feedback that a progressive flag next to a Black Lives Matter flag would dilute the message of support. In the end, they decided to do nothing. (Doing nothing is doing something, I guess). Because the organization hadn't taken any stand before, and they were unclear as to why this pressure seemed to lead them into unclear action, they didn't use their own beliefs and values as a guide. Worrying about a hostile public relations fallout is not trying to lift all spoons, and no one got fed, which, likely, is more congruent with their actual organizational values. This can change.

Perfection is unattainable, especially when succumbing to other's expectations. I like to remind people (and myself) of this: We can do anything, but we cannot do everything. At least do something.

After George Floyd was murdered in Minneapolis on May 25, 2020, a medical university posted signs stating, "Hearts & Minds Together. Black Lives Matter. We support the movement." Despite hiring its first chief diversity officer (CDO) months earlier, the organization had always maintained a stance of neutrality on anything deemed political. The following month, in support of a large #BLM rally downtown, the university announced it would hold its own event earlier the same day.

First, the CDO spoke movingly about having just relocated to the Northeast from the Twin Cities and how important it was for institutions like this one to take a stand on systemic racism publicly.

We can do anything, but we cannot do everything. At least do something.

He implied how joining the larger rally was vital. The president of the university agreed with the CDO about the need to take a stand, and then he informed attendees that the decision had been made just that morning for this rally not to join the main one, which was just blocks away. He said the university was a healthcare institution, so it wouldn't "look good" for them to join and add to a large crowd during a pandemic. At least half the participants left after that to join the main rally. It was disheartening, and it (really) undermined the new CDO too.

There are many feeble attempts to do or not do something when causes ebb and flow from media attention and when pressure to act comes in and out of vogue. I first need to say that, statement or not, if an organization is not actively doing something about racism, including conscious and unconscious bias training in the workplace and across its stakeholders and surrounding communities, then whatever its leaders are discussing is likely performative.

Regarding performative actions, posting flags or symbols should not create some kind of "Oppression Olympics" to determine what else should be included or left out. If it does, there's a larger conversation that must be had. Posting the flag or not is less important than the conversations that need to happen about the motivation to do so. This is where the real pressure lies. Being crystal clear on our motivations is the best way to deal with any complex situation that may arise.

Informed responses don't have to be complicated, but we often make this work way harder than it needs to be. I'd go as far as to say that if we were to work hard at complicated work, we might feel that we're doing work that really needs to be done and that the work's difficulty is actually doing it. It's not. For example, if I were to go out to my backyard right now and pick up Loren's axe to try to add to our wood pile, I'd be exhausted, bloody, blistered, and worn out before I'd have kindling. The effort isn't in the work itself but in finding what's needed to reach the desired outcome, in this case, smaller pieces of usable wood. Spit polishing a landmine harder will never make it the right activity even if the landmine begins to shine. Moreover, it is the wrong activity that could make a bad situation even worse if not more dangerous for those around. Trying is one thing, but you need to try that right one thing and only you know what that is.

Our organizational responses could be super clear and simple rather than too complicated. It's work we don't want to do, largely because it's difficult. We will never not need to ask the question What if X happens? Ask yourself this as well:

- Can I prepare?
- Can I learn to recognize these opportunities for what they are?
- Can I utilize the gap between a reaction and an informed response to do something in full alignment of my organization's culture?
- Can I go one step further and encourage others across my industry to do the same?

The truth is, X is happening, and you are playing catch up with everyone else. Most of my clients are terrified of going first and overly confident they aren't last. This is not a momentum building posture from which to respond. Let's keep going!

Part 3

Respond

Part 3: Respond

respond

What
about when
it happens?

Hey! There is a landmine here!

inside voice: HOLY CRAP.

outside voice:

Hey! There's a landmine in here!
Let's see what we can do!

The opportunity to respond doesn't matter if an employee isn't prepared to do so, just as pressure doesn't matter if it's not persuasive. Competitors, stakeholders, shareholders, and our surrounding communities can also be sources of pressure to do something, and they can serve as echo chambers where opportunities go unnoticed. Over the 20+ years that I've been serving my clients, I've realized these patterns overlay well with the reason for disruption. When my clients are ready, true change can happen.

If you feel prepared and are fully capable of recognizing problems you may not be experiencing yourself, then you're now ready to do your responding work. If you jumped ahead to this section, take note of that choice and back up or dig in. Here are some questions to get you ready to respond:

- Are you ready? What protocols and practices do you already have that you can tap into?

- Who can help or hurt a response you come up with, and can you bring them into the issue early? Utilizing known weaknesses, live wires, and dumpster fires is free and cheap. My clients typically rattle off the historical bottlenecks, complainers, troublemakers, and mistakes they have made that could haunt them. Can you acknowledge and invite these realities into the conversation and allow them early access, honor their expertise, to convert them into the cheerleaders and supporters you need?

- While intentionally bringing in these live wire realities into the conversation, search for the sacred exceptions, traditions, people, and exceptions, too. Sacred exceptions[3] are people and habits that have historically been too sacred and come from their own

---

3   My clients often use the terms sacred cow, elephants in the room, and hunting elephants in this stage, and I don't want to be offensive or culturally misappropriate. I should be good enough with words to come up with something else. Please use this moment to update your own language, too. You shouldn't have to think too hard to the loud voices you try to ignore and the problems that you can't address. This is a GREAT starting place because you can take the first step to doing something different.

power sources that could trip an event into a bad place when tensions are high. Can something be done in advance, or can minor adjustments be made for a higher chance of success?

- What programs, identity-based groups, or committees already exist that form a foundation for your organization?

- What is your leadership team's current capacity for crisis management? What do these key players already recognize as areas of focus or concern? What lived experiences have you or someone else had that could help you and your organization prepare?

- Utilizing outside support as scaffolding for your work could be another response protocol that helps your event be successful. Are you willing to hire professional outsiders?

- What response protocols or practice scenarios do you run through? Can you replicate them in real time? Is the plan simple enough that others can implement it? Can others utilize your idea so that it becomes an industry standard?

- What can you, your staff, your organizational leaders, your event participants, and the greater community do to monitor, listen, and learn quickly enough in order to adjust accordingly? How nimble is your plan of action?

If you feel prepared and are fully capable of recognizing problems you may not be experiencing yourself, then you're now ready to do your responding work.

If you jumped ahead to this section, take note of that choice and back up or dig in.

CHAPTER 11

Are You Ready?

When something new is happening, by virtue of it being new we have less experience (if any) to pull from and need to slow down and figure out what to do. Once we become more familiar with the situation, we can form our habitual reactions, which will make acting and adjusting to it much faster and more comfortable.

For example, Loren's 1984 Volkswagen Vanagon, known as the "Shenani-Vanigan," recently burst into flames at the end of our driveway. I was on a Zoom call in my office at home and heard Loren yelling for help. I quickly got up and ran to the front door, where all three dogs were already standing. I counted to three while trying to figure out what help was needed. In the past, this kind of cry for help had only involved dogs escaping the fence and a skunk family crossing the backyard. When I looked out the window this time, I caught Loren running down the driveway with a fire extinguisher. Immediately, I returned to my office to cancel the Zoom and call 911 to report a fire near our driveway, then ran out to the street. Loren assumed *I* would be better with fire extinguishers because of my background in crisis management, and I assumed *he* would be better at putting out fires due to his history as a park ranger. We both stood there and watched the first responders put out the fire.

Park Ranger Loren suggested I fetch a wheelbarrow for the personal effects inside the now soggy van, right after Crisis Manager Jess requested he access the van to retrieve his wallet, cell phone, and work bag from the front passenger seat. We moved quickly beyond our comfort zones and seemed stupefied by the newness all at the same time.

For two people to recognize their roles and impact in a given situation and ask more questions is a dual function that takes focus and curiosity. Reacting with knee jerk reactions is not the thoughtful response we're aiming for here. My friend Joe once told me, "You are not responsible for your first thought. But you are responsible for your second thought and your first action. That is where your power lies." Instead of filling this gap in thoughtful reasoning with confirmation bias, we can work really hard and fill it with a questioning process that allows us to be conscious of how we're choosing to respond. And we can choose to do so in a manner we can take responsibility for no matter the impact. Through asking more questions, we can start to recognize our personal patterns and make deliberate choices about what we'll do next.

Getting stuck in reaction mode can be just as harmful as getting stuck in the processing gap, because it's our duty to consciously respond. To do so, or at least to help you work toward this becoming the norm, I'm going to walk you through the six steps I take my clients through when developing a response to a crisis. Please note that you can do this work prior to a metaphorical or literal crisis.

Ideally, your leadership team is aligned, prepared, and firmly planted on a foundation that guides all responses the organization makes. Using these core beliefs and values, your organizational culture has normalized the work it takes to recognize a problem you may not be experiencing but is something you want to take on. Your organization has the resources to do it, and your stakeholders are in full agreement so you can roll out your response plan in an orderly and timely manner.

Conscious and deliberate responses are rare when it comes to the work I often do with my crisis consulting clients. We'll take each step one by one, but first an overview of what you're getting into.

As you've probably noticed by now, I like asking questions. Before any response planning can occur, let alone the actual response, I ask my clients, "Are you ready?" This is most frequently how I disqualify clients right off the bat. Prospects will often hurriedly reply, "We don't have time for this; we need to act now!" My immediate response is to give

Conscious and deliberate
responses are rare when it
comes to the work I often do
with my crisis consulting clients.

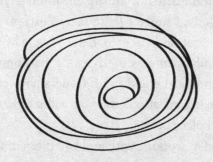

them other consultants' numbers because there's one truth that matters above all in these cases, and that is that *I* am in charge of my own sense of urgency. If they say they *are* ready, I then tell them I'm in search of any prework, succession plans, and "break glass in case of emergency" work their leadership has gone through already. I need to know whether the team has bonded into a unified team or *they* are the source of the problem — as soon as possible. If the leadership team is the problem and they don't acknowledge that, they're not ready.

Assuming we make it to the next part of the initial conversation, I ask them who will make this problem worse. I need a list of the cantankerous loudmouths with no real authority but lots of social influence and historical mistakes; for example, one client calls a situation "The Troubles" and another references "Detroit," and I need to know where the communication line breaks down, grow weak, or bottleneck. Identifying this groups of live wires should be easy and it is often the first real vulnerability, often the client needs to share. I prefer to invite, if not involve, these realities early and get them on board for a thoughtful response than have them sabotage an organization's efforts. Live wires usually turns up more sacred exceptions than mistakes, which enables me to discover the boundaries of an organization's style and culture. When not in crisis mode, I suggest these sacred exceptions be brought into a raucous conversation space to determine why they can't be touched. There's typically an interesting dynamic that connects live wires, historical mistakes, and dead ends, and if leaders have completed their preparatory work, the organization's mission will provide the answer to connecting these workplace beasts.

Once I know who I'm working with and whether I'm working within an organization that also knows who it is and how it works, we can build on this foundation. Some ideal responses won't be possible because there just isn't enough staff, time, funding, or other resources to take the best or most correct action. This obstacle can be identified and then the second-best option transparently chosen, allowing all stakeholders to know why that response is happening instead of something else.

A client I work with annually discusses each year the urgency to do advocacy work in their industry, how incredibly important and desperately needed that work is, and how their organization is exactly the one that could do it. However, stakeholders are refusing to increase dues, membership is declining, sponsorship dollars are restricted to rigid programming expectations and decreasing rapidly due to fewer members attending events, and advocacy isn't being prioritized. While this is frustrating for sure, the organization doesn't have the capacity to meet this core foundational mission, so it can't be responsibly taken on as a priority. Still, leaders say they want to do advocacy work, increase revenue, grow membership, and enhance their ability to host more events where advocacy work could take place. That *is* their response.

Where there's capacity, additional support such as scaffolding could be brought in that connects to the organization's foundation and allows it to respond on its own. It could even do so with full backing, a watchful eye, and occasional guidance and support from outsiders, including consultants, advisory boards, and other community-based stakeholders. Once they were to implement a response plan, they could set it up to inspire others in the industry to do the same or create an opportunity for mutual support. Moreover, partnering with other organizations could ultimately support more than one informed response that leaders could then replicate, learn from, and implement again where applicable. By working together, monitoring and adjusting these response plans would get easier because scaffolding-like support would become the organization's ally rather than its competitor. Each organization would then have a vested interest in the success of the community and could voice any concerns that may be seen from different perspectives, ensuring the growth and flexibility of their response plans.

At this point, you may be saying, "This all sounds great, Jess, but we're in a crisis. I don't have the luxury of planning and thoughtfulness here!" My response is that if something catches you off guard, you'll likely go into mere reaction mode, which may need to be deescalated before you and your organization can respond in an informed manner.

My clients tend to be much more open to the unknown when they're in an extreme crisis mode. At the outset of the COVID-19 pandemic, for example, workplaces figured out in less than 72 hours how they'd shelter in place. By the end of March 2020, many organizations had made decisions, monitored them, and adjusted them into an evolved response that, for the most part, worked. Yet the lives of frontline employees, first responders, and homeless populations weren't as interrupted in some ways, and we don't fully understand what they went through and are continuing to experience years later.

As the lethal threat of COVID increased, some inaccurate, short-sighted, and terrifying information was presented minute by minute, and responses were put into place that garnered high-stakes, knee-jerk reactions. We just didn't recognize it at the time. As shelter in place guidelines were lifted in some areas and not in others, organizations were weighing risk and reward against danger and loss of control, and they drafted new responses that led to more habitual reactions requiring more deescalation, including destructive and disruptive interventions. Most of my clients were now for the most part in a free fall into the unknown, yet they appeared like cool cucumbers. An ill-informed reaction was better even when the risk itself was remarkably high and there were more unknowns than knowns. This is because the entire world was in the same boat at the same time. Ignoring our responsibilities is not an option.

There is no option to ignore our responsibilities. We *can* build informed responses and make changes along the way; we just don't like doing it alone. There's also a risk of others in our industry witnessing our failed attempts (and judging us), so we don't try. We've now arrived at the opportunity to respond according to what we value the most, role model our decision processes with our stakeholders, and serve as guides across our industries who ask others to do the same.

Let's assume all aspects of your organization are in alignment and you're willingly prepared to recognize your role in making better connections with clear intentions. You're responsible for your impact and can willingly and knowingly monitor and adjust as you stumble along. You now get to respond.

Perhaps you're a lucky reader who thumbed their way to this section of the book because you currently have a fan covered in … shall we say … an unwanted substance. Perhaps the media is already calling you or you're expecting them to at any moment. You may be in emergency reaction mode. Let me just go ahead and tell you that the case studies at the back of this book could be helpful for learning how to *almost* react correctly. Feel free to learn from others' failures. Who knows, maybe you'll be a case study someday too!

In the next chapter we will walk step by step through a process to lead your organization to respond. This multifaceted approach allows you to take action knowing it may fail by responding in five ways simultaneously.

1. **Investigate** the concern and relevant situation.

2. **Coach** those involved to lead.

3. **Train** and educate others to respond again in the future.

4. **Collaborate** on suggestions for how to respond.

5. **Support** yourself, your organization, your industry, and beyond.

Once you catch your breath, you can learn to respond before the next crisis. There will be more than one opportunity for you to decipher the difference between a mere reaction or knee jerk reaction and a response. You and your leadership team get to determine what it is your organization wants to do in this world. In the in-between time, you can take the opportunity to review, reflect, prepare, and update your own organization's cultural experience for all stakeholders. You can collectively decide how you'll proceed in future responses because you have the tools to notice patterns and recognize the knowns and unknowns that are staring you in the face, searching for a fan to land on.

When pressure mounts, you *will* be tempted to just react. I encourage you to practice slowing down enough to respond from the foundation of your organization's interests and priorities. If you don't have press release templates to use as a starting place, use this moment to record exactly what you're experiencing through having no idea what you know or don't know. It will be good motivation to learn from so that you don't have to leap alone blindly again.

Until then, look at building informed, supported, long-lasting, nimble response infrastructures in your organization. Take advantage of the opportunity to disrupt what you habitually do so that you can lead the way on what you ought to be doing together.

The 5 Facets

Investigate
Coach
Train
Collaborate
Support

The 5 facets are different ways of beginning each of the 6 steps - it doesn't matter where one starts - just start... like a tandem bicycle they all need to happen together regardless of order.

CHAPTER 12

Let's Do This

It has taken a lot of therapy to say that I don't think my father handled the death of my mother very well. He was caught completely off guard, and though her battle with cancer was short-lived, it's from the outside that I can comfortably wonder how he didn't see her passing as something inevitable to prepare for in advance. But he didn't. He couldn't have those key conversations with her when he realized he wasn't prepared, and his response was to make sure that no one needed to question what he wanted when he passed.

When that fateful phone call occurred to alert me of his death, I flew home to Dallas prepared for the unknown. I knew I had three weeks of bereavement leave, but I had no idea what he'd done since our mother's passing a decade earlier, as we hadn't really talked much since then. Oddly, the first morning after my arrival, I sat in my father's office chair at his desk and opened the top drawer on the left. I knew he at one point kept his bank statements and important documents in this drawer. There, in the first file, clearly labeled in black marker, read, "In Case I am Dead." He'd thought of almost everything, down to the picture he wanted in the newspaper.

I was more prepared for the death of my father because I'd had practice with the details after my mother died. I knew things to ask for when people called wanting to help, and I knew how my dad wanted his things handled. I was left with a childhood home to empty and sell, and I'd never heard of property taxes nor paid a mortgage before. In between navigating his many girlfriends, my brother helped me empty the house and later drove off with my dad's car, which was loaded to the brim with things for his new apartment. I was left trying to figure out what to do with my parents' yearbooks. I figured it out, relied on others, made mistakes, and tried to keep my sense of humor.

No one is ever fully ready for anything, but we can get close. Step 1 of the response process was so scary because I couldn't have guessed what I would do once both my parents had died; this wasn't even a thought I had at any point in time in my life. Backing up from Step 1 is Step Zero — the land of hypothetical conversations where we bat around ideas and dream of possibilities.

As someone that doesn't have children, I have learned that it is not my place to give parenting advice. Fair. I can, however, notice patterns of my child acquiring parental friends. Some get nine months of notice others' hours, but all of my friends had hypothetical conversations about traveling while pregnant or breast feeding. Many deploy spreadsheets from research upon research about the first several years of their soon to be child's life. Then all the curveballs come into play. Some don't see twins coming while others are unprepared for terminal illnesses to strike, miscarriages, adoptions to fall through, surrogates to change their minds, and the like. We are capable of planning and throwing out the plan. The planning isn't wasted as it is learned content that may come in handy and may also not be applicable. This is why no amount of preparation for the second child truly prepared a parent for the experience, because they haven't ever had more than one kid before. You can learn, unlearn, apply, reapply, discard, and try again. To be clear this applies to plans and pancakes, not living entities you have declared responsibility for, except maybe house plants. This is precisely why I don't have children.

Step Zero: Review & Prepare

Most of my clients want to start a DEI initiative at Step 1. I recommend starting at Step Zero, which is to answer the question "Are you ready if X happens?" Again, no one is ever completely prepared, nor should any past efforts go ignored.

Think of Step Zero as having three parts, then apply each part to every X you can think of:

1. Where are we?

2. What are we?

3. Are we ready?

The answers to these questions will then lead to questions such as "Does everyone with any social power or responsibility understand the organization's desired culture?" The answer to this is wildly often no. So where do you start to get closer to this goal? Perhaps your organization has spent a lot of money on fancy consultants in the past. Did you understand their findings? Did you even read the full report? The answer to these questions is also likely no. Even more likely, you tuned out the five-minute highlight reel that a subordinate presented about the findings they skimmed through.

Review all past consultant reports, surveys, focus group findings, and customer satisfaction survey results, and look for common patterns of strengths and weaknesses to best assess what you're doing well. Yes, I said "doing well." Focusing on the positives that are real rather than those that are polished for an annual report builds momentum and allows you to keep doing something while prioritizing the unknowns that will slowly become familiar friends.

If you think your organization has the culture you want, ensure that every stakeholder along the entire value chain of your product or service feels the same. They won't. You now know something you didn't know you didn't know. It's okay. This is why you're building out a response. Yes, you may be ill-prepared to recognize a problem in advance when you're not experiencing the problem yourself, but you have to start somewhere, and you don't need to reinvent the wheel.

To develop a response instead of just a reaction, both you and those charged with maintaining or evolving the workplace culture by rolling out new initiatives need to be aware of what you collectively and most likely aren't experiencing or haven't heard before. This isn't work for the weak, but it must be done because only once you identify a consistent incongruency between what is experienced and what is desired can you focus on a common goal of being and doing better. So ask yourself this:

- What are industry partners doing around this same goal?
- Is anyone else doing this well, and if so, how?
- Do I have partners both inside and outside of the organization who have the time, resources, skills, and space to support this initiative?

If you cannot answer in unison, if you cannot confidently say that you don't know what you don't know, that you do know some of what you don't know, and that you know enough of what you don't know to collaborate on building out something new, then do not move to the next step. Start over.

Change is integrated in all formal structures and systems (such as bylaws, policies, and hiring practices) as well as through your organization's daily interactions, customs, and traditions. Collaborate by investigating, coaching, training, and supporting one another until everyone is heading in the same direction. Here's an example of a starting place:

1. **Investigate:** Review employee assessment procedures and design reporting systems to understand DEI realities in your organization.

2. **Coach:** Formalize new structures with your leadership team and ensure understanding for the whole organization. Pilot utilization of a DEI assessment in the

overall organizational mission, vision, and strategy review. The Intercultural Development Inventory*, or IDI, is a well-respected tool that assesses where individuals score themselves along a bell curve distribution of skills developed when confronted with difference. The results are reviewed individually and kept entirely confidential. Then a group review is offered so that a larger conversation can take place without any one person feeling obligated to catch up or establishing someone else as more advanced than the others.

3. **Train:** Review existing policies and reporting systems through a Q&A with leadership, stakeholders, and delegated DEI team members charged with the responsibility of enforcing internal expectations. Often employees haven't been trained in current practices, or if they have its inconsistent. Assuming everyone was on-boarded at all (let alone consistently) is an error.

4. **Collaborate:** Collect documentation for DEI procedures (including bylaws and organizational policies) you can review and refine to match your organization's culture design. Develop a campaign to communicate DEI-related processes, rationales, and outcomes to all stakeholders.

5. **Support:** Review bylaws, policies, and reporting systems. Discuss, write, and implement revisions that will align with actual practice.

Before moving on, check your "sparkly chickens" (what some people call distractions). This is an excellent time to really screw this process up before you even really get started with something new. Distractions, scope creep, or scratching everything and starting over are easier options than sitting in a series of uncovered unknowns. You didn't know. You didn't know you didn't know. Now you do. Breathe. Stay curious. When you're ready, find your naysayers, change-crushers, and dumpster fires, because there's a lot to learn from what they have to teach us.

Step 1: Seek Out Live Wires & Sacred Exceptions

It may seem counterintuitive to double down on what's going well when building out a new initiative to address what's likely being ignored, but momentum is momentum, and anger isn't a good recruitment tool. In your review of what you may perceive as realities you should've known, didn't, and now do, you'll likely uncover patterns of your office culture that you really value. Keep these going. Spread the word. Share them across your industry partners and see if they can replicate what you love and whether you can do these things even better or bigger together. Doing so will help you love the process more and, in turn, stay energized. This energy will fuel you through less exciting work while setting the tone for what's to come, and your resulting momentum will showcase your commitment to changing the bits and pieces of your organization that aren't aligned with the culture you want for your people. Your organization's purpose, plight for the planet, and ability to balance return on investment will increase profits for all stakeholders, both financially and emotionally. You may even challenge your industry partners to elevate their games too.

Marketing and communications experts love this step because when they have really good news to share, they don't have to polish, edit, or "wash" their annual reports and other assets. No more lipstick on pigs! This step can also be an important megaphone as you and your organization put stakes in the ground and amplify the organization's culture. You need to determine and then prioritize where you're currently missing the mark and then empower your people to take action. Share this discovery process across industry partners and with stakeholders to solicit pushback. This is the easiest way to find the live wires and sacred exceptions in the room. Be brave enough to listen.

Again, you and your leadership team share a commitment to face head-on what you don't know you don't know. Largely, you don't know this information because you aren't yet experiencing the problem or aren't experiencing it firsthand. It's also true that the loudmouths need to

No more lipstick on pigs!

feel welcome to share what they think you don't know and that you have to demonstrate the ability to listen to and learn from them. Trust me, they're dying to share. Turn your change-crushers, doubters, hotheads, social justice warriors, and critical advocates into invaluable resources by shutting up and listening. They may know something you don't, including the answers to questions like these:

- What and who in the organization is exceptionally scared?
- What do they think you find non-negotiable?
- Is it truly nonnegotiable? If so, why? If not, what can you learn from others' perceptions and experiences that you've missed up until now?
- What are the fears others are feeling?
- How does fear blur the recognition of a problem or unknown?

Enthusiastically seek out these voices. They offer free advice. And if their time, talent, and energy isn't aligned with your organization, they can do harm. Harness their ideas to do better so that something can change. Their ideas can both shed light on unknowns and more accurately diagnose problem situations. They can also highlight practices

check-in

A **big assumption** is being made here and throughout the book that the workplace culture and overall mission of your organization under your leadership is for good and looking to be better. This may not be the case. Honestly, you, as the organizational leadership may not know the difference. Disrupting the status quo is a starting place to being better. This means listening to those that are often ignored or overlooked. Due to their history, position, relationships, sales numbers, or whatever the reasoning to handle someone differently, needs to also be accounted for by directly addressing the exceptions. New behaviors grounded in shared purpose is the disruptive response your organization needs to be better.

and efforts that are working really well, which could help mobilize your organization's commitment to change. Review your organization's profile on Glassdoor.com, and read your customer reviews online. Be vulnerable enough to accept feedback as a gift and learn what you can from negative comments.

Years ago, when I was conducting consulting interviews at a children's hospital, I did what I always do by opening interviews or chats to all levels of the organization, from parking attendants, custodial staff, and landscapers to the highest ranks of leadership. Florence, the longest-serving custodian and a worker from the night shift, had cleaned the same section of the hospital for 38 years at the time of our interview. When I asked her what her biggest fear was about coming to work at the hospital, she quickly responded, "That one of my own grandchildren will have to come here for care." She then elaborated about how budget cuts and tensions among the nursing staff meant significant cuts of the cleaning staff. She also knew she hadn't been cleaning the multiple medical bays as well as she should've been. She was only one person doing what 30 years ago took six people to do.

Review your organization's profile on Glassdoor.com, and read your customer reviews online.

Florence filed grievances and even those anonymous patient experience cards, pointing out big cleaning jobs that needed to be done. No one ever responded with staff, equipment, or assistance. I was the first person to have listened to her in years, but she'd had the same observations for decades. I can only imagine how annoying it must've been for her to be ignored when pointing out cleaning issues in a hospital!

Can you be brave enough to listen to the free guidance that's likely been screaming at you for decades? Keep the good parts that align with your desired culture and amplify them to everyone. Then double down on your commitment to do better together.

Here's an example of a starting place:

1. **Investigate:** Utilize findings from listening sessions and analysis data to strategize and prioritize next steps with the DEI team and organizational leadership. Ideally, these findings would include participants from across the value chain of your product or service and across industry partners, including community stakeholders who come in at the ground level, work through the offering's life and disposal, and then head back to the ground floor.

   starting places for Step 1

2. **Coach:** Foster commitment to change throughout the organization through reflective coaching. Follow through on what's requested, and encourage what stakeholders, supporters, and naysayers may identify as opportunities and growth areas.

3. **Train:** Using internal and external resources, develop the skill to shift your stakeholders' perspectives about DEI to include personal responsibility, self-reflection, active listening, and building better connections rather than just mediated or facilitated conversations.

4. **Collaborate:** Identify champions of DEI work through networking and by analyzing the power dynamics within your organization. Include actual organizational charts, and document the actual flow of information and how your organizational communication processes really work.

5. **Support:** Your stakeholders are an active presence during the diagnosis to quell anxiety, build momentum, and monitor and adjust the process for lasting change. There may, however, be a need for impartial third parties to hear concerns from all people in the organization. These third parties could come from internal cross-training initiatives, parallel group members across your industry, different industries in your community, or external consultants, coaches, and trainers. Having support from third parties allows you to see your organization's capabilities and where you're going to need additional talent, resources, time, or funding to maintain whatever it is you envision.

In case you're wondering about Florence, I suggested in my final presentation and report to the hospital's leadership team that if medical bays in the emergency room were going to be taken offline due to staffing issues, then this could be correlated with a deep-cleaning schedule for custodial staff. The leadership team members who attended my presentation audibly said, "Wow! What a great idea!" Some even wrote it down on their notepads. Because the leadership team seemed disinterested in doing the long-term and ongoing work, I offered them quick fixes that lacked the punch their communications team needed for a marketing campaign. These are the same people who paid me more than Florence likely makes in a year when they could have just listened to her, but that isn't good optics. This could have been a success story or at least a "+ So Close" situation where the path to something better was in sight. Instead, we were "- So Close" and I never heard from them again.

Step 2: Build Capacity & Foundation

Once you have a clear focus, supported vision, and congruent priorities, then and only then can you build the foundation for your organization's cultural vision. For the successful development of and engagement with a cultural-change-aligned vision and a potentially industry-elevating DEI initiative, it's imperative to establish the roles and responsibilities of those at all levels of the organization. Owning the work collectively and collaboratively means more than painting a mural, hosting a 5K, or updating a tagline. It means losing the folks who can't get on board and leading those who are left. The foundational agreement of what it means to be a critical part of your organization honors those who align with this commitment and invites others to exit. Perhaps your industry partners are better fits for the employees or volunteers who are no longer serving your organizational mission, and vice versa. You cannot build the capacity toward the forecasted future you are envisioning while everything you are currently facing is sabotaging your desires.

When building capacity, there will be losses as well as gains. The same staff I worked with during 9/11 taught me this additional lesson. Half of my team were senior staff members, and the other half were what seemed to be feral weirdos who'd somehow made it through the selection process. No one really knew what to do with these misfits. My predecessor knew he was leaving, so it appeared that "Stick 'em with the new hire" was the operational plan. Within the first few months on the job, it became clear to me that my returning staff members were not only hazing the new staff but taking credit for their work.

Four months into that first professional job, I decided to have a staff meeting with the new hires. I was nervous and didn't want to set up a gossip session, so I was as clear as I could be about my observations. I was upfront that I was coming from a place of abundance and was open to ideas, suggestions, and the like to ease fears or anxiety they could be feeling as new staff members. Yet there was a problem that needed to be solved quickly. I didn't want to be a part of a toxic environment where hazing and seniority were the laws of the land. It seemed that my department was running very well, but only half of the staff were doing the work. Could we, together, foster a better place to work using only half of the staff? What kind of work experience could we create together so that we could all learn, grow, and support one another?

I've learned in retrospect that although we had the capacity to complete our work, we were missing the foundation of what our work together meant. The power dynamics didn't help. Together, over twice-baked potatoes, we looked at all aspects of our work together and figured out a way to not just complete the tasks at hand but do them in a way that demonstrated the culture we wanted to build. Anything out of alignment had to either step up or get out. Within four days, I found jobs for every senior staff member, and my scrappy and resourceful team of misfits fostered a culture that's a legacy to this day. Feral weirdo power! (I should get T-shirts made!).

Once you know what you're doing well and have listened to all the loud voices, you can clearly identify what you want your foundation to be, like constructing guardrails. From this common ideal, you can build

You cannot build the capacity toward the forecasted future you are envisioning while everything you are currently facing is sabotaging your desires.

anything within your capacity because it will be guided by your aligned priorities, such as these:

- What does success look like structurally?
- What does success feel like?
- Are there companies I want to emulate?
- Do I want to be a leader in this area?
- Are there examples of what I don't want to be like?

If they know about them, your cantankerous live wires can share all the good things the organization is doing instead of the bad. Then, you and your team can question, change, justify, or remove the sacred exceptions that show up in this early part of the response process. Think about your traditions, formal and informal, as well as habits that tend to fall under a "well that is just how we do it here" kind of mentality. Does this have to be true? I worked a job once where we had to have our timesheets turned in at Tuesday 12 pm sharp. If you were out of town or had a conflict you had to change it in order to submit the documentation at noon. No exceptions. I asked about this limitation practice to see if it was a software or staffing issue and no one knew the answer. Everyone knew Tuesday at 12 pm sharp, but not the history or reason as to why. I looked into it, and four or five staff iterations ago, the person who completed payroll would take her mother to dialysis every Tuesday. While she waited in the waiting room, she processed payroll. The sacred exception practice of Tuesday at 12 pm sharp was an outdated convenience for a staff member who no longer even worked at the organization. What other practices or habits are you doing because you no longer notice you could do something different? Who are you ignoring even though they are in plain sight? What are you devoting energy to for no apparent reason? Knowing these answers opens the opportunity for capacity building in the present moment. Once you have solid ground to build on and a clear idea of the outcome probabilities, anything is possible. Here's an example of a starting place:

1. **Investigate:** Do stakeholders know what success is? Do they even frame things as success? Work with stakeholders to determine their desired success stories. These stakeholders need to be insiders and outsiders as well as both loyal and critical customers who post snarky comments online.

2. **Coach:** Organize and plan changes with your leadership team and stakeholders to serve as listening guides. The goal is to equip others to act effectively and build systems for change, inspiring others to do the same, if not better, indefinitely.

3. **Train:** Define roles and responsibilities (new and old) with purpose-driven clarity, a timeline, accountability, and internal support. Transparently share, mimic, cheer, and showcase these internal structures for others.

4. **Collaborate:** Establish DEI partnerships, both within your industry and outside of it, that can serve as advisory councils for accountability, ideas, critical feedback, and encouragement.

5. **Support:** Actively acknowledge and seek out ways to be generous with others and accept the gift of the unknown. Some organizations will use a practice of generosity to promote safe spaces, bias response protocols, and the like.

Almost Doing Good

Once this process becomes the new normal and you habitually recognize information and experiences previously unknown to you as the gifts that they are, you can roll up your sleeves and get back to sharing outwardly what you're building and how it's going.

Being transparent and truthful about our struggles is a critical difference between a habitual reaction and a conscious and intentional response. The difference rests on a firm foundation rooted in a realistic capacity that can survive, if not thrive, in a challenge. This is why we build upward by adding additional support and accountability and leave room to reward failure as a critical step in the right direction.

Step 3: Add Scaffolding & Support

Utilizing assessment tools and retainer consulting services are some of the most common methods of providing support and structure to a new initiative. Floating just outside the walls of your new initiative building efforts is a fragile, reusable framework that would allow construction crews to get supplies where needed and keep an eye on the project from the outside. This additional structure that skims the surface of your organization's initiative is just as necessary at the bottom as it is at the top, and it must be tied to the foundation as well. As dedicated DEI champions, experienced outsiders can follow up on conversations, stir up additional ones, play contrarian, and equally support the preparation, recognition, and response pieces of your vision. Once you establish that support, you can communicate it and reinforce it.

One of my retainer consulting clients recently had me use the IDI's assessment tools with their board of directors. In this case, the board of directors had assumed there was a wide range of skill development opportunities within their ranks and had to come to terms with the opposite. The board members had similar experiences with DEI but a wide range of political views. If they could put politics aside, they'd have similar skill sets to determine the vision of their DEI initiative.

Once the board members recognized that there was a foundation of similar skill sets at the table, they felt more comfortable having conversations about the organization's DEI programs. Using apolitical language, a subcommittee of the board was able to rewrite the nominations process for leadership positions, which until this assessment had always been impacted by the board members' political views. The board also realized that the skill level of some of their members was narrower than that of the organization's membership, so they developed educational opportunities for those with differing levels of training or experience in working across differences.

Today, the board no longer plans programs they want to attend but programs that align with a shared mission and vision. Members regularly address messaging, and they document policies and procedures, lived cultural norms, and the physical aspects of the organization. And they're doing so without the same level of dismissal because they now have a deeper understanding of their and the organization's alignment. The scaffolding guides, supports, and remains, an external guiding hand to use as needed for the organization's capacity building from the foundation up. As the board facilitator, I often remind them that their answers are already in the room and that my job is to ask the questions until they know they can ask them themselves. Engaging in a lively conversation is their duty by serving on the board. Once they reach a decision, they must be the single voice for the organization. In the meantime, stakeholders can share their perspectives when insiders can't seem to see past their own experiences.

If you and your organization are facing similar challenges, here's an example of a starting place that could help:

1. **Investigate:** Develop a comprehensive communication plan that reaches all stakeholders with progress update, complete with missteps, mistakes, and dumpster fires, new learnings or ideas, progress made, and failures. The goal is to model and communicate your process, outcomes, and vision to appropriate parties at a persistent and consistent pace.

2. **Coach:** Communication matters in terms of both what's being communicated and who's doing the communicating. Guiding stakeholders to communicate about your organization's DEI initiative will generate buy-in and critique, also known as engagement.

3. **Train:** Design an ongoing plan to control consistent messaging about your organization's vision, and recruit internal trainers, participants, and content creators. The IDI, for example, requires individuals to attend an overview training before they can participate in an assessment. All stakeholders must attend a group review session, followed by optional one-on-one sessions to understand each person's strengths and where they can grow. Once an understanding is reached you can then support the larger group's initiatives in what is called an Individual Development Plan.

4. **Collaborate:** Share with, listen to, and learn from others how you and your organization could support others. Can you collectively mastermind with one another through the preparation, recognition, and response aspects of the work each person is attempting to undertake? Sharing, listening, and learning are critical aspects of building support.

5. **Support:** When designing and pushing out marketing packages for stakeholders, give equal focus to pulling in additional perspectives as well as your own. How will you intentionally solicit feedback about your process up to this point? Going forward? What kind of progress accountability can you put in place? Can you institutionalize reviews and recalls and adjust as needed?

As you develop your answers to these key questions, notice that you haven't "hit play" on your DEI program or consciously responded to anything yet. Recognize that you've already done a lot of work and that there's more to come. By continuing to ask questions, you can better align your responses with your organizational culture. Then you can consider rolling out the initiative itself and symbiotically support others moving forward.

Step 4: Replicate & Implement

The best advice I can give anyone who's struggling in their efforts to implement a new DEI initiative may seem counterintuitive: *STOP*. That may sound illogical, yet I test all elements of every initiative I assist my clients in developing. I often ask them, "What would happen if you stopped doing this? What harm is being done by continuing this aspect of the initiative?"

Every aspect of an initiative has to "audition" its way back to the response. Organizations normalize these auditions and hold them regularly as part of the building process. Some run the audition process through different groups of stakeholders each quarter, and others set up constant feedback loops to consistently gather data. The key is to assume that this will be part of the process; it can't be special or a one-off.

Deeply listening to feedback means being willing to stop doing something, even if it's your favorite aspect (Tuesday at 12 pm sharp ring a bell?). Your involvement itself is up for audition. Then, and only then, can you keep going, intentionally replicating and implementing your plan exactly the way you intended.

Being 100 percent responsible for anything is a big ask; doing so unwillingly or blindly is a dangerous ask. By generating intentional obstacles or purposeful design flaws in support of the growth of your organization's culture, your initiative is no longer lip service but the real deal, with teeth and a meaningful purpose. Most importantly, every person connected to your organization will become a part of what's being done and know exactly why.

Keep in mind that design flaws can also be perfect opportunities for adjusting your initiative before you implement it. A number of years ago, I was working with a fire chief in Montana. After our all-day session, I got to ride along with her to check on a hay baler. Though I have zero experience baling hay, I love to learn. My ride along taught me that hay baling is a multiphase process that's dependent on heat, moisture, timing, and labor. A tractor slowly pulls a baler that picks up "wind rows" of cut hay (another tool cuts the hay and then slowly twists it into these rows). The baler then weighs the hay and automatically wraps pieces of twine around it to make a bale before sending it down a shoot. Running the machine is an engine and a large wheel that keeps the rake-like fingers spinning. The large wheel weighs more than two hundred pounds and is on the side of the piece of equipment that's easily accessible. Just as I was about to ask if the wheel was a danger, I was told that this heavy wheel has a purposeful design flaw. There isn't an axle to the wheel, just a weak screw. If the hay gets too wet, the fingers pick up more than hay, or something goes wrong, the delicate screw will break instead of the entire machine getting damaged or possibly something or someone getting hurt. When the screw breaks, it stops the machine immediately, and once the screw is removed, the wheel can easily be replaced with a new screw at the center.

When any initiative of any kind is being implemented, it needs a purposeful design flaw for three reasons:

1. To stop momentum from progressing in the wrong direction

2. To inspire replication and learning from mistakes

3. To replicate the initiative using different variables that will need their own purposeful design flaws to catch necessary changes.

The best example of this that I can think of is my own COVID-19 pod and its inner workings. For the better part of a year, Loren and I worked primarily online while sheltering in place. Our two closest friends each live alone. One works as a frontline employee and was charged with delivering food to community members in quarantine and (eventually) setting up vaccine clinics. The other was 70, had retired a few years earlier, and was enjoying sitting instead of standing after having worked as a hair stylist for decades. We realized quickly that if something happened to any one of us, it would take the other three to care for each other and our dogs. Worst-case scenario, one of our homes could be quarantined and we'd still be able to help whoever else was ill.

We worked together to determine who'd go out and run errands, buy groceries, drop off meals, and the like. As vaccines became available and shelter in place restrictions began to lift, we increased our in-person visitations. Our protocols for wearing masks, keeping distance, sharing household items, and even exchanging hugs auditioned their way back in depending on the time and the person. As I began to travel again, I'd quarantine for two days upon returning home. The frontline employee and I tested every day until our pod members agreed that was excessive. Masking protocols also had to audition their way in and out, and honestly, they still do. We knew our goal was to take care of each other. We called our risk levels "spending COVID tokens," and we reviewed our process as we went along. We not only made it work but helped navigate each other's comfort levels. What we ended up implementing and replicating was our love for each other and how much we valued our pod community. Everything else was up for grabs.

I'm not going to lie. It's hard for me to think of a client who truly and regularly auditions each aspect of their initiatives and permanently includes purposeful design flaws. Typically, this is when clients seem to think they can "take it from here." Often, a project is scrapped because there's been a significant staff change and a new person has a new idea. These turns of events don't always mean the end of the program, however. I often learn from new clients about programs they've been replicating for years and aren't even sure why anymore. I know dozens of clients who have jobs funded by grants that are repeatedly rewarded to fund the job of getting the grant. Ugh.

Often, a project is scrapped because there's been a significant staff change and a new person has a new idea.

Almost Doing Good

I'm not saying that there are people in your organization who need to be fired. I'm saying that uncovering these kinds of situations through careful attention to the good, bad, ugly, ignored, and habitual, is Step 1. Naysayers will share failed initiatives that they may or may not have been part of from years and years ago. They need to be heard because there's a gold mine inside of this lived experience. No one wants an unsuccessful program to fail before it starts because it's haunted by the initiatives of the 20th century.

If you and your organization are facing similar challenges, here's a suggested starting place:

1. **Investigate:** Develop a plan for ongoing data collection, report-out systems, and ongoing assessment that's minimally disruptive to daily workflow.

2. **Coach:** Lean on stakeholders to establish ongoing internal coaches who have clear and explicit roles and timelines. Pilot new reporting systems to handle complaints and questions and be proactive in planning future initiatives. Document logic, intention, and goals for best continuity and succession planning.

   starting places for Step 4

3. **Train:** Hold on-the-ground training sessions with teams and individuals in specific areas of DEI to improve, develop, and deepen their commitment to the organization's culture.

4. **Collaborate:** Mobilize similar preparation, recognition, and response teams across your industry and in your surrounding community. These teams should meet regularly, conduct intentional listening sessions, and systematically assess each aspect of the initiative so that it can audition its way into staying.

5. **Support:** The new normal of your organization's work is to model the way for others to ask themselves tough questions. Include a purposeful design flaw that trips a response before something really big happens, such as a "See something, say something" campaign that's taken seriously at the lowest levels

before escalating. I learned in an anti-defamation league training that acts of bias (think gossip or flyers getting torn down) need to be interrupted before prejudice becomes active discrimination or leads to violence. A purposeful design flaw allows you to object to experiences that don't align with your organization's foundational culture. Full stop.

At the heart of any initiative is a conscious understanding of what you stand for, how you do this, who you serve, and why you shouldn't just close your doors. Keep your purpose, people, and the planet in mind, and your profits will follow. Your job is to prove your doubters wrong and show others how *you* are doing it!

Step 5: Monitor & Adjust

Back when I was earning my high school teaching credential, it seemed that monitoring and adjusting lesson plans was the background music to every teaching methodology we had to learn.

1. Do this best practice.

2. Assess if it worked.

3. Make changes to see whether it can work better.

What? How does something get taught as a best practice to a new cohort of educators who when doing the process slowly become doubtful of themselves? Just tell me exactly how to teach for maximum success. Wouldn't that be nice?

Just 13 days after graduating from college, I found myself in Bulgaria preparing to teach English at a science and math high school. Very quickly I learned that the American way of teaching and the culture of a classroom are not universal, nor are any "best practices." I'd assumed that the step about assessment meant evaluating the student's test scores — as if there were a universal curriculum on any given subject. What it really means is finding the answers to questions like these:

- Did I find something to try? If not, what would I need to do to try it out?
- How did it actually go? (Things rarely go according to plan.)
- What do I think about how it went?
- If I were to do it again, what would I do similarly if given a chance? Differently?
- Do I still want to try something (again)?

In a nutshell, this is the best advice I would give anyone trying anything. Learning is complicated, and any given student or classroom is complex. Add to that how department and district politics impact curriculum, standardized testing performance expectations, developing learning outcomes, and this quickly becomes an exercise in word salad. Teaching and learning are an ever-moving dance of unknowns that become knowns, and maybe competent knowns. If anything is ever set in stone regarding a best practice, it's that there isn't one. There are better ways to ask questions, be open to the results, and make informed choices about what to ask next.

All initiatives must be monitored, supported, and adjusted as needed throughout every step of the process as well as ongoingly beyond initial implementation. You and your stakeholders should be honest with yourselves when you sign up for this kind of work. It's as cyclical as it is brand-new every time you look under the hood to identify the new noise coming from somewhere in your metaphorical car. Taking this a step further, excellent record keeping and regular oil changes and tire rotations don't keep weird noises at bay, but they do provide historical data that can be monitored and adjusted accordingly.

When I go to get my oil change, I try to avoid what I call the "scream at you places." My brother worked at one of these, and I learned a lot about the reason the mechanics seem to scream so loud at each other — and me as I park my car in a bay. Some of this yelling is for safety measures between the staff under the car and those above. My brother never said this, but I think it's also a remarkably effective upselling skill. As the driver, I get so overwhelmed that I just say yes and get everything replaced. This is the opposite of what I want to happen. I want to leave, but instead the noise beats my rational mind down and builds up a pressure that seems to end only with a nod and a credit card. It's an effective process, yet it teaches me nothing about my car. I also avoid the activity, so my oil changes aren't as regular as they should be, and frankly I don't even know how often my windshield wipers need to be replaced. There's a lot of motion and noise in the shop, but it isn't about me being an informed or responsible driver. This makes me think about how a lot of consultants work with their clients and why this approach is so different. You, your organization, and frankly your industry are yours, I am just here to help you reach your goals that align with what is most important to you.

If you've made it this far in your DEI initiative, don't confuse noise and motion for progress. Remember, being busy with work doesn't necessarily mean doing the work. When a driver keeps clear records, it allows them to recognize how many miles the car gets per gallon, and if that changes they might conclude that there may be a problem. Getting regular service by miles or time allows a driver to get into a consistent habit of paying attention to their car, which can help them focus on assessing its condition and their driving experience when they'd otherwise not notice. Taking the car in can reveal problems or concerns that can be costly if not caught early and are expensive ways of learning about your car. All precautions are necessary, and none of them prevent failure.

I encourage thinking of monitoring and adjusting your plans in ways similar to car maintenance. It's a necessary step in the response process, and avoiding it can lead to confusion and overwhelm. It can even be terminal to the initiative. You have to figure out how you're going to be a responsible driver, then drive your initiative as best you can.

Between the purposeful design flaws for early detection, the regular audition cycles for testing effectiveness, and the ongoing listening sessions for stakeholders, live wires, and anyone else who has something to say, it's likely that your initiative could appear overly monitored. Your adjustments must be informed, transparent, widely shared, justified, and drenched in exciting hope that it might work. Here's an example of a starting place:

1. **Investigate:** How are you actively gathering data? Once you receive feedback, how is it communicated? Evaluated? Responded to? Is the data taken seriously? Responding is a lot easier when you know what you're replicating instead of just wanting to be liked or successful.

starting places for Step 5

2. **Coach:** Implement executive consultation throughout change initiatives so that all key stakeholders, organizational leaders, chosen live wires, and sacred exceptions understand their roles in the initiative and its most current progress status.

3. **Train:** Schedule and benchmark regular team trainings and refreshers. Consider implementing ongoing resources, such as webinars, retreats, book clubs, and team and board development sessions, to keep conversations stirring. More importantly, in these training contexts, listen for new issues, trends, or comment patterns.

4. **Collaborate:** Normalize the initiative into the regular vernacular of the organization so that it's institutionalized and organically referenced in other organizations' initiatives industry wide.

5. **Support:** Monitor change processes, coach and consult with leadership, and lead with curiosity where adjustments need to happen for all stakeholders, among the surrounding community, and across your industry.

Now that you're familiar with all the steps of the response process (including Step Zero), let's see them in action, using as an example one of my client's failed attempts to do the right thing at the right time and *almost* getting there.

Grab a pen and a sheet of paper.

Or even better, download this worksheet — and other handy tools from this book — at goodenoughnow.com/freebies

Six Steps to Outstanding Culture Change

Culture happens whether you are paying attention or not. Ongoing attention is needed to diagnose and mobilize a plan, develop an organizational vision, communicate status, test and implement, institutionalize, and monitor and adjust along the way.

VARIABLE	ACTIONS	YOU
0. REVIEW & PREPARE – Internally learn and assess your organization's current culture	Ask yourself and others, "Do we have the culture we want?" Determine whether you have the following resources available in your organization to lead a culture change effort: Time, Talent and Attention. Make sure you have a few places where there is an intersection of Time, Talent and Attention before moving on.	
1. SEEK OUT LIVE WIRES & SACRED EXCEPTIONS – Find the challenges and road blocks	What hasn't been measured before? In previous surveys what was measured? Based on the evidence that is gathered, in what areas is this organization doing an outstanding job? What is working? What is being underutilized?	
2. BUILD CAPACITY & FOUNDATION – Communicate your vision and the need for change	Reflecting on benchmarks, leaderships, and best practices, check for understanding, and identify what is possible.	
3. ADD SCAFFOLDING & SUPPORT – Build the expectation of outstanding culture into your organization's DNA	What on-going education, community building, and support can be utilized while building out your vision. How is this vision being role modeled by leadership? Stakeholders? Do organizational mission/vision, policies, procedures, etc., align to support this vision?	
4. REPLICATE & IMPLEMENT – Develop and implement specific action plans throughout the organization	Can plans be implemented across all six cultural change elements? Which are easiest? Harder? How is the impact being measured? Don't break what isn't broken!	
5. MONITOR & ADJUST – Institutionalize ongoing efforts to solidify your outstanding culture	Proactive, preemptive, check in plans to assess progress in real time to adjust accordingly to reach goals. What are new issues that need to be taken into consideration? How are you celebrating wins? Supporting others doing similar work? How are you influencing your community? Industry? Supply chain?	

Breastfeeding Station

I was contacted by a client at the state government level to help them determine what to do about a problem his organization was having that involved employee benefits. In response to (or rather, in reaction to) a new state law that mandated maternity benefits, the organization had just added them to their benefits package. Although the leaders wanted to "do maternity benefits right," what they'd implemented had evidently made things worse in the office. Interesting. I learned quickly that the phrase "do maternity benefits" was embedded into the organization's language.

I also learned that the project had been outsourced (or as I call it, "down-sourced") to Geoff, a middle manager who'd recently been promoted into the position, was single, and had moved to the state right after graduating with a master's degree. At one point during his monthly one-on-one with his direct supervisor, Geoff was given the original memo that the other leaders of this department had received. The directive was to "do maternity benefits" by the end of the quarter to be in compliance with the new state law. And go.

Geoff was not ready.

Like almost anyone would in his position, he returned to his desk to try to figure out what to do. Upon Googling "maternity benefits," he found a new trend of medium-sized office buildings installing a breastfeeding station in their lobbies. Believing this was the answer for his organization, Geoff decided to follow suit. He then asked the administrative assistant to set up an internal calendar for his floor where employees could reserve the station as needed. Doing maternity benefits was done. Check. As instructed, Geoff sent a progress report to his manager ahead of schedule, and that manager passed the good news up to the rest of the department's leaders.

Meanwhile, the employees who were using the station didn't like that the calendar title, "Breastfeeding Station," was viewable by all employees. Human resources worried that the word "breast" may not be inclusive, or at minimum could sexualize the private station.

When an HR employee returned from an unpaid maternity leave, she was elated to find a private space to pump during the workday. When she overheard others talking about the word "breast" in and out of context in the workplace break room, she suggested the station be renamed to "Mother's Room." The internal calendar name was changed by someone, and a piece of paper was hung at the station with the new name. This led some fathers on staff to ask for their own special space to reserve for privacy during the day, a decompression room of sorts. Another staff member forwarded an article to every employee that argued that not all mothers breastfeed and that the new, more inclusive term is "chest feeding."

Geoff's manager was stupefied. Not knowing what to do, management removed the station entirely before the quarterly department leadership team meeting could be held.

Problem solved! Right?

This response pointed in the right direction but missed the mark. The organization didn't cross reference the state bill with their own preexisting benefits, nor did it evaluate how it was currently serving their staff's needs. Through delegated authority, one person just dreamed up a breastfeeding station.

Perhaps all staff could've been informed that a station existed for those who needed to pump and that they could store milk in a small fridge during work hours. Announcing the opportunity for staff and

Not knowing what to do, management removed the breastfeeding station entirely before the quarterly department leadership team meeting could be held.

then allowing them to utilize it privately by asking for the scheduling link to a private "link access only" calendar would've solved a primary problem. And knowing what other similar departments across the state were doing before the election would've allowed management time to look at options in case the ballot measure passed. Once it passed, they could've asked their existing employees how they'd like to see maternity benefits discussed.

Additionally, by offering educational training to employees to showcase something new regarding organizational benefits for maternity-related needs, management could've opened a window into other existing paternity or family benefits. And by asking if current employees had any needs that weren't being addressed by the new benefits, management could've led their team to further discussions. These discussions could've uncovered what objections were coming up from employees, managers could've asked whether those objections were reminiscent of any other rollout they tried and learned from, and leaders could've checked in with their employees to see whether they needed to consider anything else.

See how being open and transparent allows for failure to have a voice, fears to have space, and needs to be attended to as aligned with the department's greater vision? Instead, this effort became too complicated and was pulled. Something was tried, but when complications arose, it was eliminated instead of understood.

So yeah, that's it.

"Oh, that's all, Jess? Geez, thanks."

Truly this is all it takes.

Communicate your wins and failures. Normalize trying. This benefits a bigger scale than just your profit margins and shareholder dividends. Sure, productivity and profitability are important, but ultimately you're trying to solve a problem you deeply care about while not being entitled to a resolution or taking credit for the solution.

We're each part of a solution to a bigger problem that addresses toxic workplace cultures that are exploiting labor to benefit a few who are already doing pretty well. Let's make the four Ps (profit, people, planet, and purpose) not a joke but a focus of our organizations' visions so that profits happen while we also address social ails harming the planet and our people. This is the purpose of any DEI initiative.

Conclusion

Good Enough Now

The key to a successful DEI initiative is the full process of preparing, recognizing, and responding. Any given opportunity can be well thought out or cause a great sense of urgency to act immediately. I remind all of us to ask more questions. Real ally, advocate, or accomplice work may not have started with all three elements, but with retrospect it's a starting place for something good.

Our knee-jerk reactions can work out for good, and the opportunity to thoughtfully respond can become a habit. The gap in the middle is where opportunity awaits. Together this opportunity can do a lot, but alone it can fizzle into an ineffective learning moment that's forgotten by leadership. To bridge the gap between a reaction and an elevated response, all three elements of the Do-Good Triangle are required.

In the bonus section at the end of this book, I reflect on a handful of case studies from my clients, friends, and family that speak to failures and *almost* successes. These examples may trigger issues of pain and harm that you've experienced in your life; that is not my intention. My intention is to use these examples as possible answers that need to generate more questions. I imagine a connection between an organization's motive or incentive to do good and the lessons they've already learned from their previous "almost-ing" attempts. Moreover, I imagine social pressure may lead to more risk-taking without proper preparation, in turn leading to failed attempts to do good. However, these failures can be stepping stones from which we can all benefit.

A collective dopamine hit can be derived together when all the ingredients are present at once. If a "do-good employee" perceives the need for advocacy, then it may have importance, even if they or a coworker haven't come forward with a harmful act. Motive and attitude are key, and they're made up of personal fears, employment stresses, and external pressures. When thinking about the code switching, shifting, and covering up that take place in an attempt to get hired and stay employed, let alone be promoted, I can't think of a time when these pressures wouldn't be present. On top of that, there's the challenge of surviving outside of work with intersectional lived experiences.

The key to a successful DEI initiative is the full process of preparing, recognizing, and responding. Any given opportunity can be well thought out or cause a great sense of urgency to act immediately. I remind all of us to ask more questions.

We can review the upcoming cases one variable at a time to learn from the answers they provide. Then we can ask more questions so that next time our intentions can move from *almost* to more successful. By evaluating examples of do-gooding gone wrong, we can learn which elements may have been present, which were missing, and how next time could be more successful.

An example of the impact of almost-ing comes to mind when I think of a meeting I had at the side of an all-women's undergraduate collegiate pool. A client asked me to meet her there to show me an example of do-gooding efforts gone wrong. Back when she was in college, she was the only Muslim student who liked to swim (that she knew of), and her classmates would make fun of her and her burkini, a swimming outfit that covers the full body. The college's response was to close the pool to all non-Muslims for one hour a week so that this student could swim in private. As she shared this example with me, I was struck by how many questions I wanted to ask about that choice.

Though this may seem like a positive response to end bullying, it's important to note a few things. First, the bullies were never addressed, nor was my client contacted about possible solutions. The policy was put into place to support her swimming access, but she never would have been able to join the swim team or even swim more frequently than this allocated hour of access. Furthermore, the Muslim swim hours were scheduled when she had class, so she couldn't use the pool without missing a class, and other Muslim students didn't understand why they had segregated swimming hours.

It may take a lot of almost-ing to find the best path forward. The key is to not just react but to take advantage of an opportunity to do good. The policy makers likely felt pressure to act quickly without really understanding the problem, what resources were available, or what the actual situation warranted. Because this situation was not a problem any of the policy writers had experienced themselves, they found a potentially justifiable, perhaps rational, solution that seemed to be a working solution. And with great and efficient speed, they made a reactive change and considered the moment handled.

My client went on to become a highly influential community member, and to this day she cites this moment at the pool as the moment she realized that to disrupt the status quo truly, something different must happen. I'm lucky to have had a follow-up moment with her because it made me feel like I could easily do something similar, feel good about it, and never even realize the impact. Yet today, decades after the incident, this amazing community leader still doesn't feel heard.

Imagine what could've been if back then my client had been listened to and her needs had been welcomed with curiosity and generosity. What if the college had set a standard for their organizational culture that harassment wouldn't be tolerated on campus and directly addressed the issue with ongoing education? What if the organization's actions had reinforced that sense of inclusion? How could this opportunity have been leveraged to support similar kinds of harassment or lack of access for other situations across higher education, religious diversity, or aquatic access? By almost-ing, we can learn from the processes that result in our answers, then ask more questions to improve the process and the answers for everyone.

Some of the failed DEI initiatives presented in the bonus case studies may have never been intended to succeed in the first place, and some may have been born of societal pressure (leaders felt their backs were up against a wall) without a real, tangible, and strategic plan (down-sourcing and under-resourcing). A leader's own mindset, emotional maturity level, and sense of self and entitlement are also required to launch any do-good initiative. When all ingredients are present, anything is possible, especially when we can learn from others' missteps and mistakes.

When I explained the concept of the "failure case studies" to a friend, she said, "You want to Monday-morning-quarterback your client's missteps and mistakes and use them for good." I think she was accurate. Even though I'm not a football fan, it seems commonplace to dissect a game play by play and make better choices in hindsight. I truly know nothing about any professional sport, so I'm just going to have to take her word for it. A postmortem analysis or even backseat driving may address this hindsight expertise, and I don't want to lose sight of the good intentions that went wrong because even if they were almost successful in the end, it is a step in the right direction.

In the military, an area I know even less about, they use something called an "After Action Review" to capture what went well and what needs to change moving forward. Similarly, facilitation practices often conclude sessions with roses and thorns, positives and deltas, and the like. These hindsight practices review, reflect, and project for next time. As another friend said, "When we know better, we do better."

In example after example, hypocrisy and irony show up as often as the unknowns do, but they also show that we can always learn to make more informed choices next time. Many of the failed initiatives did more harm by pulling or aborting the effort than by just trying in the first place. Others were misleading and harmful because the ideas came after the matter at hand had passed, making the initiative off the field of play and impossible to review solutions in real time.

The upcoming case studies provide a postmortem with real examples that didn't work out even though the chosen answer was *almost* good enough. Through reviewing them, we can build something new and better by asking more questions.

What I don't want to cause you is burnout, especially if it prevents you from trying something new due to fear of new or repeated failure. Hashing out regret, reexperiencing old wounds, and uncovering trauma is not what I'm aiming to do here, yet I need to acknowledge that sharing multiple examples to look at in hindsight may cause you to do just that. It is my hope that the good intentions of these examples fuel more good intentions in you and that they help you set yourself up for success by learning from failed attempts.

I believe true success comes from doing something different. I quit drinking in 2004, but I'm still an alcoholic. The struggle to "be" while developing into who I want to become requires intense self-work. No one else can do this work for me. Self-awareness cannot be outsourced, delegated, or shipped overseas. This is all you. You can be who you are while still being present and under construction.

The upcoming case studies
provide a postmortem with
real examples that didn't
work out even though
the chosen answer was
almost good enough.

Through reviewing them,
we can build something
new and better by asking
more questions.

Often, we think or feel that once we have X, we can do Y more effectively and that only then can we be something we yearn to be. Flipping this scenario upside down is what brings real, lasting change. We must be who we yearn to be. Being this person allows us to do something more effectively so that we can ultimately have something we don't currently possess. Our lives start with taking responsibility for who we are and how we show up, recognizing why we habitually respond the way we do, responding from where our greatest strengths can best support others, and vice versa.

You are the best tool we have to make change. If we have total control of ourselves only some of the time, then it follows that some of the time we could do the best we can with what we already have in order to influence real and lasting change.

Does this leave you feeling overwhelmed? Notice this. And try something different anyway. Sure, it would've been great to do something different long ago, but you didn't. What you're left with is today, right now. The pressure of tomorrow is enough to stop you in your tracks. The promise of tomorrow is enough to keep you going.

Recently, a friend of mine named Mike told me a story about Zoe, his soon-to-be stepdaughter. From his perspective, Zoe is as tenacious as she is resilient, and watching her develop before his eyes is his favorite part of being a new step-parent. While at a ropes course at a campsite, Zoe and her mother took on a multilevel challenge course. The first level was easy, but Zoe struggled to get to the second level. She stopped and went back to the first level, deflated and disappointed. Then she turned around and saw her mother crest the top of the fourth level and progress to the fifth. In that instant, Zoe figured out how to get over to the second level and kept climbing.

Mike said, "It's not just that she tried; it's that she never quit trying to try."

Can you do that?

Never quit trying to try.

For real change to ever happen, we must do something different. Real, lasting change, in both our personal and our professional lives, starts with (re)reclaiming our responsibility for how we show up. If we start individually, I deeply believe that others will join us and follow. Collectively, we can role model the way into the unknown — into the different — so we don't have to go at this alone. All that's needed is to shift our mindsets toward recognizing that we need to do our own work if we're to truly role model for others the space needed for their whole lived experiences to be present.

We are good enough now.

If you enjoyed reading this, please leave a review on Amazon. I read every review, and they help new readers discover my books.

Part 4

Bonus Material

Almost-ing Case Studies

Loren was trying to add oil to his truck. He asked me to help him by holding the funnel so he could pour a quart from a five-quart container of oil. The funnel was wedged into the space, so I assumed he must've been doing his own oil change once and the funnel had slipped, making a big mess. Maybe it wasn't even him. Maybe he just heard about a case when this happened. Maybe he thought ahead and decided it was a possible outcome, so now he holds the funnel no matter what.

Similarly, I save my documents every time I get interrupted, and every time there's a section break or I stop typing and think for a second or two, I hit Save. While writing about this habit of mine, I've saved twice already. Why? Because back in college, late at night with a due date looming, I lost a paper. Unfindable. No do-overs. No Ctrl + Z redo. Gone.

Things like these typically happen only once before a behavior changes. For the same reason that pilots practice crash landings, we retain the experiences that caught us off guard: to inform our future experiences. We know what action to take next time because we learned from previous experience. Sometimes we sputter with excuses and perfectly logical reasons for why we can't respond differently or mustn't change. This happens to all of us. Yet we can also surprise others and ourselves by diving into something completely different, even unexpected; it all depends on the situation at hand.

Being "Good Enough Now" is about doing the best we can with what we have some of the time because it's better than doing nothing all the time. The key is to recognize that disrupting to do good isn't just about what we know or think, nor even about how we respond to or apply pressure. The most disruptive way to do good is to do something different that builds our own practices and inspires others to do the same slow and intentional process of ongoing work. It's the work of curiously looking for what we don't even know we don't know, becoming less defensive and more comfortable with the unknown itself, and making authentic, informed, and intentional guesses about what to do next, all while generously being transparent of our vulnerable failures.

It takes courage to use the tools we have at our disposal to make better and more authentic connections with others. Maybe you're already great at this, yet there's always room to make an improvement. Some connections are solid; others are not. We all have work to do. Making choices about how we want to show up balances two elements: risk (cost) and reward (goals). If we work to habitually make real, lasting change in the form of better, authentic connections with generous sharing, vulnerable listening, and genuine curiosity, we have a goal or reward for our efforts. When we're truly being our full selves and allowing others to do the same, there's less of a cost to us all. Perhaps, then, this isn't an act of courage but an act of living.

What's holding you back? There's a time and place for reflection and response, and you must become aware of your comfortable patterns to decide who you are and how you show up in your relationships with others. Doubting ourselves, thinking negatively, fearing failure or success, criticizing others, participating in negative self-talk, procrastinating, people-pleasing ... if these lived experiences and voices in our heads went away, imagine what we could do. With hindsight, we could look back and see why we didn't do something or where we went wrong. We could recognize where we drag our feet, bite off more than we can chew, or allow momentum to be in control. Much like fraud,

With hindsight, we could look back and see why we didn't do something or where we went wrong. We could recognize where we drag our feet, bite off more than we can chew, or allow momentum to be in control.

if we have a personal motive or incentive fueling an internal pressure or have experienced outside pressure, we may do something that's uncharacteristic for us or our organizational culture, even when it's for good. This is disruption.

It's true, too, that we could do something outlandishly good with the right motive or incentive. At times we may experience external pressure from current events, trends, personal experiences, or relationships and be compelled to do something. These "doings" don't always go as planned, and none thus far have toppled systems of oppression in all forms, yet they can still be the right things to do. As with successes, failures can be defining moments because they help us strive to develop, improve, and get better.

Let's review some examples of moments, choices, and plans to do good and with hindsight identify where these clients could've been more successful. In some, we'll review which particular element(s) of the Do-Good Triangle was present and see whether we can identify where we would've used our gas pedal differently. Remember, almost-ing is easy, yet it's not fruitful unless we stay curious, are generous, and allow our authentic selves to be vulnerable about our failures and lived experiences.

Let's get to work.

In some case studies, we'll review which particular element(s) of the Do-Good Triangle was present and see whether we can identify where we would've used our gas pedal differently.

American Red Cross

The rise of the AIDS epidemic in the 1980s led to the 1982 requirement that blood donors complete a questionnaire prior to donating their blood. Until 2019, gay men who engaged in anal sex weren't allowed to donate blood under any circumstances, even if they were HIV negative. As of 2022, the overall ban has been lifted, but now anyone who has engaged in anal sex with a new partner within three months of the scheduled blood draw, regardless of either's gender or sex, must wait. All donations are screened for HIV regardless of the donors' answers on the questionnaire.

Almost. If all donations are screened for HIV (and other sexually transmitted infections such as syphilis and hepatitis), then the original policy perpetuates homophobia and the stereotypes that gay men are more susceptible to HIV. The 2022 policy is a more equitable one that with changed attitudes about high-risk sex led to a waiting period rather than a complete ban. Removing only one group of people who may or may not engage in anal sex is a form of irrational discrimination. Even if well-intentioned, this long-standing policy significantly limited the amount of blood donations across the country and beyond, even if it seemingly made sense at the time.

Defeating Anti-Gay Marriage

Arizona's 2006 Proposition 107 was the first anti-gay marriage bill defeated in the United States. This defeat was successful largely because it centered around the impacts of its passage on Tucson's domestic partner provisions that guaranteed benefits for those in a domestic partnership even if they weren't legally married. Specifically, this successful campaign focused on an elderly heterosexual couple who would lose veteran-related benefits if they were to marry. The measure was narrowly defeated, 52 to 48 percent.

Almost. In politics, some argue that a win is a win. I like to use this example to show how our intention to do good can still lead to harm. Utilizing the details of personal and family benefits, along with the complicated lack of clarity around corporate benefit packages, the loss of such protections or coverage certainly got heterosexual voters' attention. The fact that Tucson already had a local ordinance protecting all domestic partnerships and that passage of this new bill would take away a right for residents of the state even attracted folks from outside Tucson. The visual use of an elderly straight couple in marketing pieces and television ads heightened fears to such a level that the measure failed in a state that had already passed bills that didn't recognize out-of-state gay marriages.

Utilizing this confluence was a strong political chess move, as two years later Arizona's attitude toward gay rights swung to a more progressive one. However, it's important to mention the local community harm that occurred between those "trying to win" and those in the queer community watching their actual rights and access to benefits be overshadowed by a chess game that centered on straight people's fears.

Accessibility

A large metropolitan city's commissioner passed a wide-sweeping ordinance to change bathroom signage to read "All Users" for any renovation or new builds across the city. Allowing for any single occupancy restrooms for any renovation projects or new builds addressed the need for gender-neutral bathrooms, but it also affected caretakers and children who needed privacy but had to be in the space at the same time. However, no educational plan was connected to the ordinance, let alone an accountability structure. Consequently, these extra duties fell to the volunteer LGBTQ+ employee resource group (ERG) to develop, evaluate, and implement.

This same LGBTQ+ ERG hosted a panel called "Beyond the Binary" in the one classroom building without any all-gender bathroom options. This program was particularly designed for students, faculty, staff, and community members who identified as outside a gender binary, and it was about discussing ways the institution was working toward inclusion of all community members regardless of gender identity or expression. Yet participants had to pick either a women's or a men's restroom while attending the event.

Almost. These kinds of events involve a lot of details, planning, and foresight. Emphasizing particular aspects of inclusion that are often then overlooked due to planning details, limited options, and lack of experience is particularly ironic. Needing sign language interpreters, closed captioning, accessible ramps, wide aisles, translators, safe changing rooms and bathrooms, and parking, as well as honoring everyone's pronouns, is just the beginning of accessibility issues when planning such events. Understanding these commonly overlooked needs is essential to supporting an inclusive mission to do the right thing.

Typically, these oversights are blamed on a lack of need or knowledge about accommodations or an inadequate budget. Yet it *is* possible to state upfront what accommodations will and will not be included at the event, and budgeting in advance for accessibility can also mitigate deficiencies. Many accommodations are cost free or nearly so as well. Clarity is kindness.

Water Tracing

While I was working at the University of Arizona, the geocaching club was working alongside the coroner's office to identify where deceased immigrants were located in the surrounding Tucson area deserts. The students organized water stations and drop-off and refill trips in areas that connected these spots on the map, assuming this was a pathway others would be following. But upper administration specifically ordered that this club's activities cease because of "potential danger" the students could be facing. As the advisor at the time, I believed that the biggest concern was negative press associated with anti-immigration that could hurt admissions if the word got out to potential students or new hires.

Almost. Almost two decades later, I admit that this case study still really bothers me. I think it's an excellent example of doing good with the resources someone already has because it combines all elements of the Do-Good Triangle. Yet it was canceled due to two facts and one belief: 1) the institution was located close to a politicized southern border in a desert, 2) immigrants crossed this desert on foot under extreme conditions that often resulted in death by dehydration, and 3) this danger would sufficiently deter others from coming. This is beyond an incongruency with the beliefs and values of the institution who instead refused aid to the weakest who needed the most assistance.

Bring Your Whole Self to Work

A large global technology company leads by instilling a handful of tenets that set the tone and expectations for their employee and customer culture. One phrase the company uses quite frequently (and not in a mocking manner) is, "Bring your whole self to work." After a recent hateful post was shared, this tenet was reviewed internally and found to be unclear, inequitably understood, and derived from the founders' secular and progressive agendas. The leadership team had assumed that the meaning was clear and consistent to all. These are two different assumptions. After I conducted over one hundred listening sessions, it became clear to me that the phrase had created wildly different experiences for each employee, team, department, region, country, and time zone. Some heard "Bring your *whole* self to work," while others heard "Bring your whole self to *work.*"

Almost. The company's value statements were consistent with the beliefs and values that the founders had brought to their new venture. And though they're proud of their global growth over the last few years, this tiny team of original leaders still lead the organization as if it were small. At the time of the negative posting, they were "off grid" at a leadership retreat and 23 hours behind the employee who posted it. Even if they'd been at their desks, the founders had outsourced internal communications and would still have had to be told about the post.

Furthermore, no one in leadership globally identified with the political party that supported the ideology behind the post, and they may have missed the connection between the internal post and an internal group. The listening sessions revealed that some employees took the stand that their "whole self" was welcomed and that this could foster conversation among their peers. The leadership team eventually identified that an employee's whole self is welcomed *if* it aligns with the leaders' secular and progressive stance; otherwise, the emphasis should be on work. What an example of do-gooding gone astray.

Crowdsourcing

When tasked with renaming a campus building of a prominent law school, why not ask the public for suggestions? The timing was just after the school had been named after a supreme court justice's passing, and the crowdsourcing was to assist with proposing names of historical, progressive leaders and then putting finalists up for a community vote.

No one expected this opportunity to spread so quickly nor that it would be picked up by "right-wing bots," as evidenced by the thousands of hateful contributions that flooded in within the first 24 hours of the poll's opening. Initially the upper administration supported the intention and process behind the crowdsourcing naming idea, but they completely shut it down by the end of day two. More than a decade later, the student affairs building is still named "Student Union Building 1," or "SUB 1," and there's no inclination to rename it without a donor stepping in to purchase naming rights. There will likely never be another public crowdsourcing initiative on this campus.

Almost. This reminds me of the people who squash what seem like new ideas because "Back in 1972, something like this was tried and it failed." With that line of thinking, a great idea that could be developed differently or managed better goes awry and is never tried again.

There's a fine line between micromanaging an open forum and creating an unmonitored space for feedback. It's also hard to stay on top of weblinks and the like because they can "go viral" in a second with today's technology. I'm not sure I'd even have a thought about ruthless "spambots" mucking up the process to the point that the effort of polling for a new name would be squashed. When combined, motive, incentive, outside pressure, and personal attitudes and rationalizations are not enough to do good. This is, however, an excellent example of trying that can be a lesson encouraging us to try again.

ERGs

Employee Resource Groups (ERGs) are often created to support initiatives in the corporate environment. They're intended to motivate and support underrepresented employees in an effort to both build community and offer internal programming that addresses a specific issue, as well as to educate allies. Multiple ERGs may exist and may have conflicting meeting times, forcing an employee to pick an identity instead of being their whole self. These groups are often led by volunteers with little or no connection to top leadership, and they're woefully underfunded, if at all.

Almost. Having a "safe space" for marginalized or underrepresented employees develops communities of support that have a direct connection to retention and even make an impact on recruitment efforts. However, leaders who implement them often have to support themselves and end up doing the heavy lifting of educating coworkers. Many of these coworkers rarely support an ERG's programming because they think it's a space for "others." This also imposes upon these same others the role of providing free education on top of their job responsibilities. ERG leadership and programming can be seen as a distraction from an employee's responsibilities and reflect negatively on job performance. In the end those burdened by structures of social injustice become sometimes doubly burdened by these initiatives.

Women's ERG

A large global tech firm I worked with was having a lot of race-related issues among their staff. One of the most powerful instigators was the leadership team of the women's ERG, which was made up of three White women who took their roles very seriously. Outside the ERG, the women were middle managers from three different countries, but together, they focused on the lack of women in the tech industry globally. Among topics central to their agenda were increasing the recruitment and retention of women in the workplace, establishing pay equity, and including pregnancy, miscarriage, abortion, IVF, maternity leave, and breastfeeding stations in their benefits packages. This agenda critically overlooked women of color, who were being significantly underpaid compared to their White counterparts and even less represented than White women. Nonbinary and trans employees, both White and of color, felt even more silenced by the advocacy of the women's ERG leadership because their focus was representative only of cisgender women.

Almost. This is an excellent example of how motive or personal incentive can be crystal clear and still miss the mark. ERGs are often problematic to begin with because they're often underfunded, underutilized, and run by overworked volunteers. Among other issues, these volunteers often have negative performance reviews, not to mention having to choose an identity when becoming involved in one ERG over another. And yet they attempt good work. The three White women were personally incentivized to have their concerns addressed because they were trying to solve problems for other women just like them. Meanwhile, their actions alienated other members or potential members, leading them to ultimately shut down their collaborative efforts to improve the workplace for all on a global level.

Menstrual Supplies

Wanting to be more inclusive, a health clinic began to put menstrual supplies in all bathrooms for patients and staff to use or take with them. Over time, the supplies were stocked only in restrooms identified as "Women." This practice didn't acknowledge that anyone, regardless of declared gender, may have need for the supplies. Nonbinary and transmasculine visitors, for example, might still menstruate or know someone who may need supplies. Moreover, in the same bathrooms, the urine collection instructions were still gendered as men's and women's instructions even though they were in gender-neutral bathrooms.

Almost. The motivation to have all-inclusive and gender-neutral spaces in all settings, not just healthcare clinics, is rooted in good intentions. However, we rarely think outside of gender when making gender-neutral accommodations. The incentive to make all patients and their guests feel welcome gets replaced with typical binary-gendered habits. The result is that the initiative falls flat for the very people it intended to benefit.

To offer menstruation supplies is to offer them to whoever needs or wants them regardless of a person's gender identity or expression. By defaulting to typical habits, the most vulnerable visitor, someone who's not perceived as a person who may menstruate, would have to out themselves to gain access to free supplies. The people most impacted by these oversights are the very people who don't fit into a binary system, and they're likely the only people who'd notice the hypocrisy.

Single-Use Restrooms

A division chair was reflecting on a situation when it had become clear that there were no safe restrooms for nonbinary people on campus. As part of the solution, the chairperson began discussions with administration and facilities people about what was needed and suggested changing the sign on the single-use restrooms to reflect that usage was not restricted by gender. These particular single-use restrooms, long designated as "Faculty Women" and "Faculty Men," were accessible only with a key. Faculty pushed back on the updated signage, saying, "Where will *our* restrooms be?" In the end, the signage on those single-use restrooms was successfully changed despite faculty objections. However, these restrooms always remained locked! Anyone wanting a private restroom had to go to the division office and ask for a key.

Almost. The division chair learned to be specific and explain fully when advocating for change. The power dynamic between faculty and students needed to be accounted for in this conversation, and it may have become a cultural entitlement they were used to. Was there another option for faculty to privately use a restroom on campus or in the building? Was there a rational reason for these restrooms to remain locked throughout the day or during the times when the building was being used? Could cisgender faculty, nonbinary faculty, and students all have used this space? If the bathroom doors of genderless, single occupancy bathrooms could lock from the inside, couldn't they have remained open unless in use?

Talking Stick

A facilitator of a large group was looking for a meaningful and simple way to wrap up a five-day intensive training for sexuality educators. She put the 50 participants in a large circle and decided to use the "whip method" by asking each participant to reflect briefly on the entire training experience. Recently, a dear friend had given her a foot-long stick that was beautifully carved into a phallus. To continue with the theme of the training, the facilitator decided to use the phallus as a "talking stick," passing it along to each participant in the circle to signify the holder as the "talker" to be honored for their moment of sharing.

Handing it around to the first few people went fine, despite the chuckles. Then it was placed into the hands of a Native American participant who said as she began to cry, "I'm sorry. I cannot do this. This is not a 'talking stick.'" The facilitator stopped the process, dispensed with the prop, and the group completed the exercise. Afterward, as people dispersed from the closing circle and the training, the facilitator apologized to the participant for her ignorance and presumption.

Almost. This facilitator shared with me, "I've never fully recovered and feel very humbled in my cultural ineptness. I've long been very interested in Native cultures and practices, but my fascination isn't enough to ensure I don't appropriate them for my shallow purposes." In hindsight, she could identify both her motive and mistake. Some could also argue that a co-facilitator should've checked this assumption before the closing activity started or plan the closing activity in advance and in a more thoughtful manner.

I challenge us all to take a moment to sit with this. Both the motive and the impact of such a mistake are real. Being clear on her intentions and taking responsibility instead of being defensive makes this a crucible moment in the facilitator's life. This doesn't mean that she'll never misappropriate a culture again, but it does mean that this experience has shaped how she questions herself and her plans moving forward.

Introvert Hire

A small youth service organization specifically recruited an introverted professional to serve its introverted young members better. The overly extroverted staff and organizational leadership did nothing to change the culture or staff engagement expectations to support the new hire. Moreover, coworkers mentioned during a meeting that this candidate had been hired because of their introversion. This happened following the busiest programming season, during which other workers had been fired for not being outgoing enough.

Almost. Recognizing that current services are inadequate for some users and then specifically doing outreach to recruit a staff member to work on this programmatic weakness is certainly doing good. Not informing the new recruit that their introversion is what attracted the hiring committee to them due to this heightened awareness of service needs is a missed opportunity for communication. Expecting this new hire to then fit into an office culture that knowingly focuses on more extroverted kinds of engagement is contradictory at best. The positive intentions of inclusion and the employment performance rationale don't align and don't support efforts to increase services and improve the organizational culture for all.

Cannabis

The legalization of cannabis in California was a highly motivated act with financial and medical incentives. Here in my local community of Humboldt County, California, since the legalization of cannabis I've noticed an increase in housing availability and a decrease in rent inflation, as legal grows must meet permitting requirements while illegal growers are less likely to set up shop in local residential neighborhoods than before, driving up prices and sucking up the housing supply. Knowledgeable dispensaries opened, and the resulting huge influx of innovation opened doors to many new small businesses.

However, the permitting process to legally grow is bureaucratic and understaffed due to an underestimated amount of interest. While waiting for permits to be approved, illegal grows still occur; many are so large that the small businesses can't compete. In addition, working conditions for illegal and permitted grows in Humboldt County, for both small- and large-scale cannabis indoor and outdoor farms, still aren't being monitored. Grow farms have no HR departments, and the environmental impact of grows has no checks and balances for sustainability initiatives or state-level requirements. Moreover, most folks in state prison for cannabis-related crimes are people of color, while primarily White people are now profiting off the newly legal activities. Whether individuals are incarcerated or not, the cannabis industry hasn't been decriminalized. Therefore, criminal records, tax evasion, trafficking, and other illegal activities still occur inside the now legal industry.

Almost. It seems to me that the sales tax, permitting fees, and state-level profits were strong incentives to permit farms, but the rest of the plan wasn't really thought out thoroughly. Where housing rental rates are decreasing, small businesses are now being pushed out of limited commercial spaces to make room for more profitable cannabis dispensary businesses wanting tourist-heavy locations, which is impacting all local businesses. As of the end of 2022, Idaho, Wyoming, Kansas, and South Carolina are the only states without some level of cannabis decriminalization or legalization.

Office Furniture Hierarchy

A university client had recently changed their administrative offices to an open floor plan to encourage collaboration and teamwork and to align with a less hierarchical organizational structure. The large office space had three walls of floor-to-ceiling windows; the fourth was all windows to the internal hallway with a main set of double entrance doors. As students and staff entered the office, they could see bright colors, gathering spaces, and a colorful mural that noticeably stated, "Welcome all and all welcome." The space was a collection of stand-up desks, docking stations, desktop computer stations, high tables, conference tables with wheeled chairs, clusters of half-walled cubicles, and meeting spaces with doors and half-windows along the perimeter.

Upon closer examination, a hierarchy was present based on how much privacy was allotted to each office space, regardless of the level of confidentiality involved in the employee's role. The most tenured folks had private offices, stand-up desks with both desktop and docking stations, flexible furniture arrangements, and internal access to private meeting spaces. The middle managers, however, were clustered together in a half-wall cubicle "farm" with wheeled chairs, and they were surrounded by the newest entry-level employees who stood at desks or sat at tables with open docking stations. The office had a number of student employees and interns who used whichever spaces were open during their shifts and then packed everything up at the end of the day.

Almost. Open spaces and flat organizational charts allow for transparency and clear lines of communication by decentralizing power concentrations. Perhaps unintentionally, furniture was selected by tenure and projected a sense of permanence or lack thereof. Those with the lowest job status had the least stable workspaces, other than being tethered to a landline here and there when they were sitting in the unwheeled chairs. The incentive for permanence and privacy was unconsciously immortalized in the very space where the stated intention was just the opposite.

Hair

"Ooooo, your hair looks cute!" said a White woman senior leader in the organization to a newly installed Black woman president while reaching out to touch the top of her head. The two women had gotten along well since the president's start on campus. The senior leader assumed that their friendly, playful, and silly communication style had made it possible to be this comfortable with the new president, and she'd forgotten to think about the racial and power dynamics between them. The president immediately returned a serious look and called the senior leader into her office a few days later to discuss the situation.

As she came out from around her desk, the president invited the senior leader to sit as well. She explained, "I am telling you this because I truly believe you are not aware of what you did. You never, ever, ever touch a Black woman's hair, especially when she's your campus president." The senior leader apologized as clearly and simply as she could, offering no excuse.

Almost. So much attitude and rationalization to unpack here! There's a pattern in which many think to themselves, *We're friends; therefore, our identities don't matter.* This thinking is as harmful as it is casual. A person's lived experiences never "do not matter." A White woman touching a Black woman's head can reverse the power dynamic of a president and a subordinate.

The president calling her employee into her office is also something to think about. Few people get called into this office, so when the new president came from around her desk to sit next to a long-standing employee for some "feedback or advice," the dynamic shifted again. The senior leader who shared this example with me was still grateful years later that the president spoke to her "alone, non-threateningly, and clearly" because the President recognized that the senior leaders just didn't understand the impact of the mistake.

It's imperative to mention here that hair itself is policed and subjected to policies. In 2019, for example, the Creating a Respectful and Open

World for Natural Hair, or CROWN Act, was created to ensure protection against discrimination based on hairstyles (primarily racialized hairstyles) by extending statutory protection to hair texture and protective styles such as braids, locks, twists, and knots in the workplace and public schools. CROWN should not have to exist, yet it does nor has it been passed on a federal level as of this writing. Clearly, racism and the belief that only either straight or curly hair, not kinky hair textures, are clean and professional are concerns in many workplaces.

Hygiene and professional standards are rooted in White supremacy; otherwise, there wouldn't need to be a law protecting the way hair naturally grows on or out of the human body. As a White woman with often atypical hair colors, I'm amazed by the number of people who touch my head or ask question after question about how I get my hair the color it is. (I typically respond, "I have a checkbook.") I know that I have a degree of fascination with differently textured hair than mine, styles my hair can't or won't do, and the flexibility of wigs and extensions with which I have no experience. But my ignorance about hair does not give me permission to ask invasive questions or touch someone's head.

Making policies that deem what's clean or professional based on what we're used to isn't even a nice try. We can do better. And by "we" I mean those, like me, that benefit by position or other privileged identities. As of 2023, 23 states and more than 40 municipalities have passed the CROWN Act.

Membership Demographics

I've worked with two different groups that are primarily for lawyers, fiduciaries, and law firm partners and found an interesting pattern showing up regarding membership demographics. Associations with paying members typically have applications for joining the organization and renewing dues. On these applications, demographic information — including age, race, sexuality, gender, tenure, ability-related accommodations, locations, and education — can be gathered as either required or optional questions. This information is typically used to set recruitment, retention, nomination, and leadership pipeline goals as well as internal measures for programming or volunteer recruitment. These questions are often even used by human resources to ensure that issues such as benefits, furniture, and dress codes align with a new employees' needs. In both cases, in these organizations made up of legal professionals, I had to explain that these were not illegal questions to ask and that they were the foundation of any strategic plan they were following.

Almost. These organizations (and probably many more) felt external pressure to have a strategic plan that increased the diversity of membership by X percent, but they didn't have baseline data regarding four issues: 1) the current diversity of membership, 2) a working definition of what diversity meant regarding their membership, 3) how they were going to increase numbers from an unknown, and 4) by when, let alone why. At first, not having a plan was worse than having a bad plan, so it was time to fix a bad plan. However, the leaders didn't want to "make" anyone participate even though they'd stressed that the plan was important to their organization and not just lip service.

No Surprises

Two tech companies hired me through their equity committees or a similar initiative run through their human resources departments. In both cases, these select groups of employees wanted to roll out DEI-related programming and solicited my assistance to both facilitate the training and design an internal program. There was one caveat: no surprises.

Before the two companies could pick which workshops they wanted and in what order, I test-piloted or "auditioned" each of my webinar offerings to multiple groups and one-person audiences, both in person and virtually. I explained the order that worked best, and I was overruled. Then I offered listening sessions to gather pain points of employees and offered an assessment tool to quantify the learning needs of staff. These options were controversial because I couldn't provide transcripts of the listening sessions before they were offered, nor could I present assessment results prior to giving the assessment. The leaders also recommended that I develop PowerPoint decks and submit them for approval before any town hall meetings, open discussions, drop-ins, or facilitated conversations.

Almost: First, no diversity consultant was harmed in either of these instances, and I have a therapist! Second, this is a great example of the external pressures — usually from top leadership — to produce results, fix problems, and be omnipotent even with new issues or dilemmas that have never been faced before. The elevated need to know is typically indicative of past initiatives' failures, and leaders tightly control future work to avoid past problems. This is internal almost-ing using external tools and resources. It should come as no surprise that requesting scripts and practice rounds, as well as approving artifacts such as PowerPoints for facilitated conversations, isn't about doing good; it's about leaders controlling expected outcomes due to performance pressure.

Leadership Forum

An international organization made up of first responders (police, EMT, fire) built out a leadership pipeline program through which more seasoned leaders could mentor up-and-coming staff from around the world. This program was also set up to allow the new leadership to work on global projects to create new and innovative systems, protocols, and procedures while learning best practices from around the world. The program would be four years long, culminating in an annual conference where all participants would come together to create and innovate as well as learn from a consistent leadership curriculum.

The certification board supported the initiative but asked that it be self-funded at exactly the same yearly level regardless of participants or current events. The curriculum would also need minor updates in case internal policies changed, but the program was expected to give the exact same experience to each mentee or program participant to meet the leadership expectations of lobbyists, legislators, and global first responders.

Almost. What? A single curriculum was to be designed, monitored, adjusted, edited, and implemented year after year in the exact same manner? And with first-, second-, third-, and fourth-year participants, groups of mentors, and presenters to a global audience to inspire creative and innovative ideas but with no funding?

It is important to monitor and adjust programs as living and breathing experiences instead of prioritizing a "one size fits all" program that splits the middle and hope for the best outcome. Please stop doing this.

Gift Cards

A university's response as COVID-19 hit was to quarantine students in empty residence hall rooms when they tested positive. These students couldn't leave their rooms for meals, so they were given gift cards to purchase groceries out in the community. Eventually, a single staff member was selected to take orders, shop, and deliver these groceries because the quarantined students were often too ill to shop for themselves and there was worry of endangering the public.

Almost. Instead of worrying about the community catching COVID, the university should've worried about the nutrition of the students in their care and the health and non excess use of workload of the employees. We often worry about protecting the least weak variable. This staff member was given no additional funding, resources, time off, or even PPE supplies. Now three years later, she's still the "go-to" solution for these kinds of situations, and her full-time position seems to rationalize these responsibilities as "other duties assigned." Perhaps the initial thought was that the gift cards could be given to other students to make the purchases for the ailing students, but there was a mandatory shelter in place protocol. Meanwhile, ill students were isolated and given a gift card for comfort.

Fast Fashion

As consumers, we rarely think about the value chain that goes into the life cycle of an article of clothing. We — and I mean me — make quick, impulsive purchases and often wear clothes once, or never. "Fast fashion" generally isn't good for employees and laborers making the article of clothing, the environment sourcing the materials, or even the location where the article of clothing may end up on the planet. I could write a story about the good I'm doing by supporting businesses and then donating clothes to those in need. These donations may land locally in the hands of someone in need, but then how long will they last? If they aren't taken up locally, then these items could be recycled or repurposed and end up in the hands of someone selling them from giant piles on corners of economically disadvantaged communities or in resale shops where clothes are sold by weight.

Almost. I know, I know. It's hard to think all the time. The good news is that once we practice something, it becomes a habit. What does it really mean to buy something? Own something? Get rid of something? Perhaps supporting harmful systems isn't our goal, but it happens because we forget what our original goal was. If there wasn't a market for disposable items, they wouldn't be made. The image of starving and homeless children running around streets begging for change or food scraps in fraternity bash shirts is hard to forget, and if I'm being honest, hard to always remember.

Hikshari' Trail

Though named locally by tribal leaders, the Hikshari' Trail is often referred to as the Eureka Waterfront Trail in my hometown. The trail is a long bike path that was installed along the bayfront for recreational use. Before it was installed, several hundred people lived in tent cities they'd formed several years prior. These houseless women, men, children, pets, and belongings were removed with a week's notice. The area was then cleaned and landscaped, and the pathway was installed with benches, bike repair stations, doggie bag stations, public bathrooms, and water fountains. This land is also protected by the Environmental Protection Act.

Almost. This experience was particularly hard to watch unfold, and it's an excellent example of a complicated opportunity. Watching from my patio window while the tent city was removed, and at times witnessing "boobytraps" that lit the tents on fire rather than someone taking them away, was a moment of privileged reflection that I will never stop thinking about. My family is excited to use the Hikshari' Trail for dog walks and bike rides, as well as for gaining bay access for kayaking. It's middle- and upper-class folks like us who are being catered to and encouraged to enjoy nature while judging those that are using the space to survive and disregarding the environmental impact of anyone's presence in the space regardless of intention.

Acknowledgments

Words tend to eject themselves out of me like a scene from the *Aliens* movies, but this project has been much, much more than I bargained for.

I first had an idea about case studies when I had a conversation with my mastermind group, Thom Singer, Gerry O'Brion, and Eliz Greene. When I gave an example from a past client, Gerry challenged me to write out more examples like the one I shared. Before I knew it I had hundreds of examples.

Later, I asked on Facebook whether other folks had any examples of DEI initiatives that went worse than doing nothing, and I received lots of examples. To respect their privacy and/or job security, I've altered their examples, submissions, ideas, and experiences. Oddly, there isn't a single example that couldn't have been submitted by someone else, because these are universal dilemmas. I do, however, want to give special thanks to the folks who talked me through some of the details of their ideas as well as those who "played almost" with me as I wrote this book. Thank you for the ideas, questions, details, and suggestions. And thank you to those who've talked me over ledges and under bridges and made this part of the book much stronger: Paul Artale, Debbie Caselton, Ric Chollar, Melissa Glass, Sarah E. Holmes, Kathy Klotz-Guest, Brian Mistler, Ann

Murdoch, Caitlin Nye, Donn Peterson, Mir Plemmons, Kaylee Rosa, Carolyn Segermark Llewellyn, Ant Stroud, and possible others that I'm missing here.

For longer than I would've thought possible, I played around with 50+ case studies as I looked for some order or structure to them. Interestingly, though I was super clear on the concept of almost getting something right and seeing these examples as a step in the right direction that didn't work out, I couldn't see the pattern in *why* they didn't work out. Until I did.

I was doodling in my notebook while standing at a gate at Denver International Airport when I randomly thought of something from my MBA program. (Feel free to diagnose me as whatever you need to, but I mostly doodle in geometric shapes, so as I was drawing triangles I remembered Cressey's Fraud Triangle.) When COVID-19 hit, it took me less than a month to enroll into the one-year MBA program at the local university where Loren teaches. I feared breaking sobriety, but with a partial tuition waiver and a program I could complete within a year, it sounded like the affordable structure I needed. To my Cal Poly Humboldt professors, Ramesh Adhikari, Dove Byrne, Jaime Lancaster, Humnath Panta, Li Qu, David P. Sleeth-Keppler, Tyler Stumpf, and Josh Zender, you did the best you could with what you had as we all punted into a virtual world. None of us knew what we were getting into, and I need to acknowledge the effort you put into something that really taught me a lot. Thank you.

One thing I learned from school is that I'm a project manager! To my study group, a.k.a. Breakfast Club Members, Jace Baldosser, Aaron Friedley, Ranjan Hatch, Deanna Hahn, Muranda Kozlowicz, Evonna Lintz, Michael Magana, and Monica Roybal, know that I know nothing about so many things. Thank you for getting me through the finish line.

Another thing I'm really good at is big ideas. Back to Cressey's Fraud Triangle. There was something there that mesmerized me, and I couldn't figure it out until I was at that gate in Denver, doodling on the side of my notebook while thinking about 50+ failed DEI attempts. If I haven't already dated myself as a classic Gen Xer, this was my *Working Girl* moment of Trask Radio. I posit that the Fraud Triangle, used to this day to avoid unethical accounting practices though based on rationalization, opportunity, and pressure, doesn't just explain committing corporate crimes. It's the basis for disrupting what's expected simply because someone can — they have the mindset and the access, and they feel the need or want to do something unexpected, in this case illegal acts.

I looked at the case studies through this disruption lens, and suddenly they sorted themselves out into three clear categories where the initiatives seemed to react from one position but not respond from all three. Then the book began to form, and the Do-Good Triangle of prepare, recognize, and respond came to light. This is the formula to truly disrupt expectations for good. Any attempt for good matters, even if it *almost* gets there. Remember, it's always the right time to do the right thing — even when it doesn't work out.

Unfortunately, two hundred thousand words later, I could no longer excavate clarity on my own. It took a small village of patient eyes and minds to tell me that the stream-of-consciousness, mind-castle-of-an-albatross book wasn't a book — yet. Thank you to Nancy Harrington, Ken Wachsberger, Steve Piersanti, Owen Fitzpatrick, Craig and Liz Wruck, and many others for wading through that first mess. And for making more than one hundred thousand words vanish so that the real ideas can shine through, thank you to Jill McCarthy, Marcus Foote, Barb and George Handyside, Loren Cannon, John Sileo, Traci Brown, Ruth-Hazel Hammond, Beth Ziesenis, Jennifer Meliton Eisenreich, Anne Bonney, Pat Dwyer, Gail Rubin, Candace Doby, Angela Prestil, Carl Seidman, Stacey Crowley, Aaron Gregory Smith, The Real Housewives of Coney Island (Courtney, Tina, Stacy, and OG Meg), Jen Grace and her team at Publish Your Purpose, Nancy Graham-Tillman (who drew the short stick), Sam Demma, Alyssa "Twist" Light, Joe Gerstandt, Jesse Mejia, Alana Hill, Amy Waninger, Bernadette Smith, David Rowell, Devin Thorpe, Donna Mack, Glen Guyton, Greg Jenkins, Judith Katz, Justin Jones-Fosu, Lauren Dike, Lisa Gray, Lisa Jenkins Brown, Lisa Koenecke, Tony Chatman, Anton Gunn, Camille Chatman, Rhodes Perry, Lois Creamer, Summer Stark, and Mary Helen Conroy.

Speaking of ideas, no one can know what they do or don't know without the help of others. Josh Packard and Megan Bissel, from what's formerly known as Inclusive Solutions, pulled a process out of me that I didn't know I was using. Delta Gamma Fraternity taught me what doing good can mean, and from every artist I've taken classes or walked around galleries with, I learned how to accept feedback and welcome new and differing ideas or suggestions without being too attached to the original pathways. Moreover, I learned how to know what I'm *not* changing, even when it's dark, misunderstood, or outright not accepted by others.

This is the diversity book I needed to share with the organizational leaders I work with, watch struggle, and support while the world seems to be on fire. Your efforts aren't in vain. I see you. Together we can solve anything, make anything, and do anything—just not everything.

Realizing that my learning curve happens in real time of me causing pain and suffering in others is the motivation I need to keep trying.

Index

Almost Doing Good

About the author

Perhaps it's her Texas roots, but Jess Pettitt, MBA, M.Ed., CSP, believes that to really thrive in this world, you have to ride two horses—one of giving and one of receiving. For Jess, the giving horse is her passion for service, and the receiving horse is the high she rides entertaining audiences.

For almost 10 years, Jess rode one horse by day, serving as an administrator in student affairs for university Diversity and Inclusion programs, and the other by night, performing and hosting three times a week doing stand-up in New York City's most popular comedy clubs (ask her about George Carlin's nickname for her or sharing an eggroll birthday cake with Bob Newhart).

Eventually, Jess discovered she could ride both horses at the same time in the same career, and a speaker in the DEI space was born. Now, nearly 20 years and half a million audience members later, Jess gallops from coast to coast delivering her "Good Enough Now" message to anyone willing to take the leap toward creating a much more inclusive (read: much more effective) organization.

If you'd like to discuss bringing in one of the funniest speakers you'll ever hear to deliver actionable content on everything you've ever wanted to know about Leadership and Diversity but were afraid to ask, reach out to Jess today.

jess@goodenoughnow.com
917-543-0966 cell

NOTES

Made in the USA
Monee, IL
20 October 2024

67456322R00148